The Round Towers of Fingal

Their Hidden History

GERARD RONAN

25 BLIANA YEARS

Comhairle Contae Fhine Gall
Fingal County Council

Also by Gerard Ronan:

The Irish Zorro.
William Kelly of Portrane.
Sophia Parnell-Evans: Feminism, Politics and Farming in 19th Century Portrane.
Margaret Evans: Poet of Portrane.

FOR CLIONA AND ELEANOR

ACKNOWLEDGEMENTS

I owe particular thanks to Gregory O'Connor, archivist at the National Archives in Dublin for his guidance and patience, and to Glenn Dunne at the National Library of Ireland and Josh Hilliard at Independent Newspapers for permission to use their images. My thanks also to Carol Quinn at Pernod Ricard, for permission to use the photograph of the Power's Whiskey Bottle Tower.

Especial gratitude is also due to Helen O'Donnell, Senior Executive Librarian with Fingal County Council, without whose assistance and guidance this book would not have been published. Last but not least, is the debt I owe to my wife, Cliona, and my daughter, Eleanor, for their eternal forbearance and support.

CONTENTS

THE ENDURING MYSTERY

NO CHILD EVER left an Irish school without being able to recognize a round tower. Ask them, even in adulthood, to describe their purpose; well, that is another matter entirely. Most will tell you a tale of fleeing monks scurrying into a tower, pulling a ladder up behind them, and then giving the proverbial finger to the pursuing Vikings. The Viking swords and spears, they might also tell you, were no match for the one metre thick walls of the tower. It is a tale beloved of children, and of the teachers who revel in telling it.

But of course, it isn't true, at least not entirely. Only the most desperate would choose a virtual chimney as a place of refuge from a pursuer who was burning their homes. And yet, occasionally, some did. The first recorded mention of a round tower, in fact, comes from the year 948, when the tower at Slane was burned by raiders. Crammed with holy relics, distinguished persons, and 'the best of bells', it was as efficient a death trap as was possible to construct in those days should your pursuer decide to set fire to the door. Hardly surprising then, that they all perished.

The tower at Slane has disappeared, as one might have expected of a limestone structure that was deliberately incinerated. Just 40km down the road, however, in the town of Swords, a tower of similar age and construction survives. This strategically situated conurbation, once considered vital to the defense of Dublin, was burned on no less than 11 occasions over a span of 150 years, and yet the round tower survives pretty much intact. How, you might well ask, can that possibly be?

Ever since Christian monks brought Roman technology to Ireland in the 7th and 8th centuries, the builders of ecclesiastical compounds had known how to burn limestone to produce lime. The small stone churches they had been building for almost 200 years had used this lime to cement the stones together. As a predominantly limestone structure with a timbered interior, the tower at Swords would have been particularly vulnerable to fire. And yet, it still stands.

Could it be that the tower itself was never attacked because the people of Swords had learnt the lesson of Slane? Indeed had the round towers been intended solely as places of refuge it is unlikely that the ancient round towers of Fingal would have been built at all, let alone left standing, as all, without exception, had been constructed within Viking controlled areas and with the tacit approval of the ruling Viking elite. By the time the first towers were being raised in Fingal, in the middle of the 10th century, the Vikings had already become a permanent part of Irish society. The Irish aristocracy had, in fact, been using them as allies, mercenaries, and trading partners for almost a century.

The Vikings controlled much of north Leinster at

this point, including the towns of Howth, Swords, and Lusk; towns whose monasteries had prospered under Viking control. Indeed, such was the Viking domination of the area that it quickly became known as *Fine Gall*, literally 'kindred of the foreigners', a name that survives to this day as 'Fingal'. The coat of arms of Fingal County Council still features a Viking longboat and raven, recalling the *hrafnsmerki* flown by Viking chieftains of the 9th to 11th centuries. The increased visibility of a tower in the landscape, in any case, would have been more likely to advertise the presence of a wealthy monastery than conceal it; as likely to attract a raid as a travelling pilgrim. Hardly the go-to design feature of an architect focused primarily on safety!

So, if the primary purpose was not that of protection from marauding Vikings, what was it then? Why the sudden reach for the sky? To find the answer to this we must take the annals at their word. In these ancient manuscripts the towers are quite literally described as bell houses (*cloig teach*) and, from four windows that looked towards the cardinal points, the canonical hours would be broadcast. In this manner, the towers mirrored the Islamic minaret, from where the idea may well have been borrowed.

Just as the *muezzin* would call the Islamic faithful to prayer, the Celtic Christian *aistreoir* would ring his bell. By dividing the day into regular periods of religious observance the towers of both religions functioned as early public timepieces, encouraging the discipline of timekeeping long before the invention of the mechanised clock.

That it should have been bells that broadcast the hours in Ireland, rather than the human voice or bronze trumpets, probably had something to do with the peculiar affection the ancient Irish reserved for these metal instruments. Copper-brazed quadrangular iron bells were first manufactured in Ireland in the 7th century and continued in production until the 10th.

Indeed, so many hand bells from the early years of Irish Christianity have survived that we can be pretty certain of their widespread use in the regulation of monastic time, punctuation of the liturgy, and the animation of religious ritual.

Celtic Hand Bell

By the 9th century, however, as bigger and better bells began to be made, the practice evolved of every Christian church having one: a practice that was apparently at its most popular in those regions of Europe where the influence of Irish missionaries was at its strongest. To this day the influence of bell-ringing on the development of structured timekeeping can readily be seen in the fact that the old Irish word for bell, *clocc* or *clog*, is reflected in the medieval Hiberno-Latin *clocca*, the French *cloche*, the German *glocke*, the Dutch *klok*, the Swedish *klocka,* the Danish *klokke,* and the English 'clock'.

Sometime in the early to mid-tenth century, however, at a time when the Vikings were already well settled in Ireland, something strange began to happen. The largest and most influential monasteries began to ring their bells from the tops of a tall circular 'bell house'. But to what end?

Perhaps it was a natural consequence of the monasteries' success? As their religious communities grew ever larger, so too did their need for ancillary services. The commercial opportunities offered by their size and wealth attracted all manner of tradesmen to settle close to them, making the monasteries the focal point of rapidly expanding urban centres. One could easily imagine a need for the bells to be heard beyond the rooftops or tree line, or of an ambitious abbot wanting to announce his authority and cast a subliminal influence over as wide an area as possible.

We may never know for certain why the first towers were built, just as we may never know much about the type of bell or bells that the round towers once housed, or indeed how they were rung (the bells have not survived, presumably because the metal was considered too valuable not to be re-cast when their use as bells had been exhausted). Whatever it was that prompted the development of these towers, it was obviously considered too mundane to be recorded. Construction and destruction were recorded in the annals, but little else. It is just one of the mysteries that have yet to be solved.

One mystery that *has* been solved, has been that of the doors, and their positioning 2-4m above the base of the freestanding round towers. Contrary to popular belief, the positioning had nothing to do with Viking raiders, or indeed Irish raiders for that matter, and everything to do with physics. The oldest towers were generally built of uncut rubble on extremely shallow foundations that would have been vulnerable to storms without some form of strengthening. They gained their stability by packing the lower 3-4m of the tower with soil and stones, effectively building the bulk of the foundation above ground.

It is for this reason alone that the doors were situated so high above the ground, and not because it allowed the fleeing monks to pull a ladder up after them to escape from Viking raiders. Simply put, a door at or close to ground level would have weakened the entire structure and left it vulnerable to collapse. In Fingal, the doors of the round towers at Swords and Lusk appear close to the ground purely because the ground has risen over the centuries to meet them.

Excavations during the 1990s found postholes close to the door of some Irish towers, suggesting that wooden steps were often used to access the doors rather than ladders, but inside the towers, from the door upwards, several wooden and highly flammable floors would have been constructed that *were* accessed by ladders, the number varying from four in Swords to nine in Lusk. The cap or roof, in its original state, would have been made of corbelled stone and conical in shape, such as exists on the tower at Clondalkin. Restoration of damaged towers, however, has often meant that current caps have been constructed of more durable material and may not reflect either the height or shape of the original. The tower at Lusk is a prime example of this type of 'restoration'.

As mentioned already, perhaps the most unique feature of the round towers is the nature of their foundations, which were constructed by digging a shallow trench of less than a metre in depth which was then filled with unworked stones. Upon this shallow foundation walls were built up with rubble and mortar and constructed with a slightly tapering incline so that they leaned in on themselves and gave the tower extra solidity.

But why round, rather than square or rectangular, like the stone churches that usually accompanied them? Were the builders clinging stubbornly to an atavistic fondness for circles, Celtic structures having been predominantly built this way before the arrival of Christianity? There are certainly aerodynamic benefits to be gained by circular structures in high winds, but could it also, perhaps, have been a taste for the exotic?

The artist-historian, Hector McDonnell has speculated that the Irish Round Towers were a local attempt to imitate the first free-standing European bell towers, such as that erected in Ravenna in the early tenth century, and which in turn are believed by some to have been inspired by minarets of the North African coast. These Italian bell towers were predominantly circular in shape and the oldest of them, the bell tower of the Duomo/Basilica Ursiana, is thought to have been built roughly contemporary with the appearance of the first round towers in Ireland.

One proposed explanation for this coincidence is that Irish monks on a pilgrimage to Rome had witnessed and copied the tower at Ravenna. Indeed, it was common for Irish monks to undertake the *Peregrinatio pro Christo* (Pilgrimage for Christ) and to go into a wandering exile on the continent of Europe. It is not impossible then, that at least one Irish pilgrim to the Vatican may have witnessed the tower at Ravenna or the frescoes in the Old Saint Peter's Basilica, which held depictions of the round towers of Rome, Jerusalem or Antioch, all of which were still extant in the eighth century. The idea appears unlikely, but no more so than the appearance of the towers themselves.

As for function, it is not impossible that some towers may, on occasion, have served as watchtowers, at least in those places where a clear view was afforded from the topmost floor. However, as the towers were not always built in locations with a clear view, this again would have been more a matter of opportunity than design. There is some literary and architectural evidence for the storage of holy relics in the towers. The height and thickness of the walls would certainly provide greater protection from fire, both accidental and deliberate, than the thinly walled churches below. Their function, however, had always been, first and foremost, to house the monastery's bells.

Whatever may have triggered the sudden explosion of 10th century tower building in Ireland, the towers quickly became fashionable and came to be seen as a reflection of the status of both the monastery and its aristocratic sponsor. Given the state of lime mortar technology at the time, the building of such towers would have represented an expensive and labour-intensive project that would have taken as many as eight months to complete. Taller than they ever needed to be for a bell-ringing function, they represented the Gaelic equivalent of the great cathedrals of mainland Europe. It seems likely, therefore, that they were, to some extent, designed to be seen as much as heard.

One of the most curious things about the Irish round towers is the lack of obvious architectural precursors. They just seem to leap out of nowhere. Towers, of course, had been around since the time of Babel, but what makes the Irish round tower distinctive, is not just that it is circular and free-standing, but that it emerged without any apparent evolution and persisted with so little change in design over so prolonged a period of time.

The introduction of scaffolding, the use of pulleys and hoists, not to mention the architectural knowledge necessary to compensate for the unusually shallow foundations, represented technological advances unseen in the country prior to the building of these towers. The subtle degree of tapering necessary to stabilize the structure and the innovative construction of the foundations largely above ground, also represented engineering advances unseen prior to this. And yet, these innovations appear to have come about with any obvious history of experimentation.

*The bell tower of the Cathedral of Ravenna
(late 9th- early 10th century)*

Being so long removed from the sphere of Roman influence, lime mortar technology had arrived very late in Ireland, but its use had still been evident since the 7th and 8th centuries in the construction of small rectangular religious buildings. Tall circular dry-stone walls had likewise enclosed large forts throughout the island since the Iron Age. And yet, despite 200 years of building with lime mortar and even longer of building circular drystone walls, there had been no tradition of constructing any tall free-standing structures that were even remotely like these. Then suddenly, in parallel with the second Viking age, new architectural expertise appears. The knowledge arrives fully formed and, apparently, specific *only* to the task of building a round tower.

To this day the round towers of pre-Norman Ireland represent remarkably uniform feats of engineering and design but, being so totally at odds with the indigenous building traditions of their time, and without any known precursors, it was perhaps to be expected that some historians would begin to doubt that they could have been constructed by the native population.

The complete absence of prototypes begged the question: had the engineering knowledge necessary for their construction come from abroad? Had it come, perhaps, with traders from Anglo-Saxon England, where stone belfries had existed since the early ninth century and octagonal Roman lighthouses, such as the 'Pharos' at Dover Castle, since the first? There is solid archaeological evidence for an Anglo-Saxon presence in Dublin long before the arrival of the Vikings in 841, but little else, as of yet, to support the theory.

In 1725, Dr. Thomas Molyneaux argued that the towers had to have been of Danish origin, but there is nothing in the Danish archaeological records of the 9th and 10th centuries that even remotely resembles an Irish round tower. In 1832, one Henry O'Brien asserted that they were relics of phallus worship, for which theory he was awarded the sum of £20 by the Royal Irish Academy! And then, in 1866, at a public meeting in Clondalkin, a certain Caleb Palmer and his friend and colleague, John Darling, set forth several arguments claiming them to be of Eastern or Phoenician origin, in a direct challenge to George Petrie's assertion that they were buildings of the early Celtic Church.

Petrie, wisely, didn't respond and has subsequently been proven to be correct. That said, it is perhaps worth noting the discovery, in the 19th century, of a Phoenician seal in Dundrum in County Down. The seal, which read *'Belonging to 'Abd'eli'ab, son of Shib'at, servant of Mittitti, son of Sidqâ'*, was dated to the 8th century. In the 1970s, furthermore, the skull of a Barbary ape was found during excavations at Navan Fort in County Armagh. The skull was dated to 390-20 BCE, which overlaps with the latter period of the Phoenician empire and a time when the species was largely confined to North Africa. All of this would appear to suggest trading links between Ireland and North Africa that had endured for over a millennium prior to the construction of the first round towers. Palmer's assertion, therefore, though erroneous, was perhaps not as outlandish as it might first have appeared.

The construction of the towers is currently accepted to have been commissioned by the early Celtic church, but the source of the engineering knowledge required to build them remains a mystery. To this day many historians continue to adhere to the principle of *ex nihilo, nihil fit* and look outside the country for influence rather than consider the possibility of a moment of native genius. There exists in folklore a tradition that the towers were designed and built by a famous 6th century architect from Turvey in Donabate known as the Gobán Saor, but Gobán had died several centuries prior to the construction of the earliest towers.

The final mystery surrounding the round towers concerns the manner of their construction. Why so high? Why so little variation in design? Why did the towers not evolve? Was everyone building to a master plan or sacred text? Why were so many towers built so close to 100 Roman feet in height when, in some places at least, a smaller tower would have functioned just as effectively? Why was the height of the towers so close to being twice the circumference of the base? Was there some forgotten significance given to the mathematics underpinning the architecture? Or was it simply a reflection of the height of the tallest native trees? And why, when the skills needed to build the towers could so easily have been put to other architectural uses, were they not? Had the same plan been merely copied and re-copied throughout the ages? Had the Irish builders lacked the architectural skills or imagination to adapt, or had they simply no need of permanent forts and castles?

If the knowledge and skills necessary to build these towers *had* come from abroad, why then did it not come complete with other foreign architectural advances such as the ability to build an arch? After all, cathedrals had been built on the continent of Europe for at least 500 years prior to the construction of the first Irish round tower, and at least double that had elapsed since the golden age of Classical Greek and Roman architecture. Was it solely the *idea* of a tower that had arrived? These and many other mysteries remain to be solved.

SOPHIA EVANS AND THE WIDOW'S TOWER

ADJACENT TO THE grounds of St Ita's Hospital in Portrane there stands a round tower on a prominent headland that looks out across the sea towards Lambay Island. It is, perhaps, the most visible and most famous of all the round towers in Fingal and, for a long time, its silhouette loaned a rare distinction to the peninsula.

When the tower was being built, in 1843, the only sounds to be heard at its base would have been the cries of the herring gulls or the occasional bellow of a stag. On a windy day, perhaps, the sound of waves crashing into the cliffs at Tower Bay might have carried this far. It was an isolated and scenic spot, overlooking the graveyard at St. Catherine's church, and an ideal location for a moment of peaceful contemplation.

The deer park has long gone, St. Catherine's is no longer visible from the tower, and the psychiatric asylum has closed. But the tower remains, aloof and authoritative before the same expansive sea view that greeted its construction. Unlike the surviving round towers of ancient Ireland, however, the Portrane tower does not mark the site of a monastic settlement. It recalls, instead, the love of an extraordinary woman for her husband and the lives of two families who found themselves at the heart of Irish literary and political circles during a period of social upheaval throughout Europe.

Sophia Evans erected this replica round tower in honour of her husband, George, who for nine consecutive years had served as M.P. for the county of Dublin in the British House of Commons. These days, it equally stands as a monument to herself and for a time, it even carried the epithet of 'The Widow's Tower', before the widow, too, faded to obscurity.

Sophia Evans was born Sophia Parnell, the only daughter of Sir John Parnell of Avondale in County Wicklow. It is not known exactly when she first met George Evans but it was most likely during, or soon after, her visit to Paris in 1802. George was a frequent traveller to the French capital, where his family lived in enforced exile on account of his father's involvement in the 1798 rebellion. He was also on friendly terms with Sophia's brother, William Parnell.

Sophia's path to adulthood and marriage started with a funeral. On 6 December 1801, her father, Sir John Parnell, having just returned from a debate in the British House of Commons, died suddenly of a stroke at his town house in London's Belgravia. One of the most shrewd, intelligent, and respected politicians of his day, Sir John was a former Lord of the Treasury, Chancellor of the Irish Exchequer, and one of the wealthiest men in Ireland. He left his children more than adequately provided for and heirs to a political legacy that each, in their own way, would struggle to come to terms with.

Following a brief period of adjustment to their newly independent circumstances, William and Sophia, then in their early twenties, decided to live a little on their inheritance. Sailing in the wake of friends who had departed the previous November, the siblings set out for Paris, the signing of peace preliminaries between Britain and France having seen hordes of curious nobility racing to the continent to experience for themselves the aftermath of revolution.

Their older brother, Henry Parnell, recently married to Lady Caroline Elizabeth Dawson, also travelled, albeit separately, and was never recorded in his siblings' company during the trip, or even within the same social circles. The younger Parnells, as liberal as their elder brother was conservative, held unconventional political and divergent religious beliefs. Not having a political career to protect they could, and frequently did, indulge their intellectual curiosity. Sophia even contrived to underscore her newly acquired independence by infiltrating a circle of radical society women who would forever influence her view of the world and, indeed, of herself.

The war of 1793-1801 had effectively closed France to tourists. During that time the French monarchy had been swept away by revolutionary forces that, in their turn, had been brushed aside by Napoleon. With newspaper reports proving an unreliable witness to the events of the decade, those educated and wealthy enough to do so decided to take advantage of the peace and go and see for themselves. Their morbid curiosity satisfied, they then reverted to type. Their 'grand tours' quickly became more about pleasure than education, and vast sums were spent by the wealthiest in entertaining themselves and their guests. The Parnells, sufficiently well-connected to mix in such company, travelled with Lord Peter King, 7th Baron King of Ockham, and socialised frequently with Lord Stephen and Lady Margaret Mount Cashel.

Under the ideology of the 'separate spheres', gender roles were clearly divided at this time. Women were consigned to the private sphere of the home and family, and men to the public sphere of economics, politics, and industry. As a result, wealthy families rarely educated their daughters alongside their sons, and women were raised to be wives and mothers, to manage servants, and make prim and 'delicate' conversation. They were not expected to have political opinions, or display knowledge of science and philosophy, let alone opinions that might contradict or embarrass their husbands. An 'intelligent woman', to many, was considered a contradiction in terms.

The only female in her family since the age of three, Sophia Parnell was an uncommonly tall and slender young woman of prodigious intellectual ability. Denied the educational opportunities of her brothers, who had been educated at Eton and Cambridge, she slaked her thirst for knowledge in the family library, and in her private reading developed a love of Voltaire, Hume, and Gibbon: reactionary and atheist thinkers that few governesses of the day would have dared to introduce to an impressionable young lady. Forceful in her liberal convictions, she represented something of a societal risk to prospective suitors and, despite several London 'seasons' and a sizable marriage portion, she had, at the age of twenty-two, still to attract the attention of a compatible marriage partner.

Lady Margaret Mount Cashel, on the other hand, had married purely for position and now found herself trapped and trammelled in an unhappy marriage with a man whose political views were the polar opposite of her own. The Irish diarist, Katherine Wilmot, a travel companion of the Mount Cashels described Margaret as both 'socially charming and attractive, highly cultivated, upright and refined'. She also described her as 'harsh to her children, a freethinker in religion, and imbued with what were then the most extravagant political notions'. In the young and impressionable Sophia Parnell, Margaret Mount Cashel found what she could never find with her husband – an intelligent and sympathetic companion.

Margaret Mount Cashel's 'extravagant political

notions' had largely been sown and watered by her childhood governess, the proto-feminist writer, Mary Wollstonecraft. An early campaigner for women's rights and the author of *The Rights of Women.* Wollstonecraft had tutored Margaret for just a single year, but her influence was so profound that Margaret would forever look upon her as the surrogate mother who had 'freed her mind from all superstitions'.

Margaret King Mount Cashel (1801)

As a writer in her own right, Margaret Mount Cashel had also, much to the annoyance of her husband, composed pamphlets for the Society of United

Irishmen during the 1798 rebellion and befriended the infamous Lord Edward Fitzgerald. During her stay in Paris, she had also become acquainted with Robert Emmet who, less than a year later, would be executed for leading a rebellion in Ireland.

Sophia's future father-in-law, Hampden Evans, was also a friend of Fitzgerald and was visited by Emmett in Paris during this time. It is more than probable, therefore, that his family was also friendly with Margaret Mount Cashel – a woman whose political leanings had once been considered so extreme that she had no sooner settled into married life in Ireland than she had incurred the suspicion of the Government.

Throughout their time in France, Sophia and William Parnell travelled widely with the Mount Cashels, the siblings charming English and Parisian society alike with their wit and intellect. Impressed by their intelligence, Katherine Wilmot, described them in her diaries as a 'very extraordinary pair of beings'. Lady Margaret Mount Cashel, a decade older and heavily pregnant at the time, was especially enamoured with them, so much so that, in June of 1802, following the birth of her second son, Richard, she asked William Parnell to stand as godfather.

So closely were Sophia and William said to resemble each other they might as well have been twins. They were also said to be intellectual equals. The influential liberal politician, Charles James Fox once described William as 'one of the best as well as one of the cleverest men I ever knew' and Katherine Wilmot described him as a young man with a 'small face and features, colouring cheeks, and smiling eyes.' Portraits of the time show him balding prematurely in his early twenties. His sister, by all accounts, was no more fortunate in her appearance.

Resentful of a society that placed greater value on looks than intelligence, William, at the time of his visit to France, was putting the finishing touches to his first novel: *Julietta: On the Triumph of Mental Acquirements over Personal Defects*. It told the Cinderella-like story of a humpbacked child and her struggles to find respect and affection in a family obsessed with feminine beauty.

William Parnell c.1810 by John Comerford
Image courtesy of National Gallery of Ireland

At the crux of this novel, the aged and ailing Lord Marsham advises eighteen-year-old Julietta on how an intelligent woman might make herself the mistress of politics, economics, and all the sciences, without becoming insolent, contemptible, or untrue to herself. Julietta, under his tutelage, would eventually find happiness courtesy of her persistence, guile, and intelligence. Published later that year by Joseph Johnston, the book reads, in retrospect, like an instructional fable for his sister.

Their liberal leanings notwithstanding, the Parnells were not beyond a bit of celebrity gazing. They even managed to wrangle an invitation to the Tuileries, Napoleon's official residence in Paris, where they were presented to Madame Bonaparte (later Empress Josephine). Katherine Wilmot also attended, William Parnell and Lord King having travelled to Versailles to collect her for the occasion. The Parnells may also have dined with Napoleon and Josephine at the great dinner party of 5 June 1802, as they regularly attended such functions in the company of the Mount Cashels, whose attendance that evening was noted in Wilmot's diary.

During her stay in Paris, Sophia frequently shared the company of many of the city's independent-minded and influential *salonnières*; intelligent women, like herself, who appeared to live a life of intellectual freedom and influence. Most notable amongst her acquaintances was Sophie de Condorcet, widow of the late French philosopher and mathematician, Nicolas de Condorcet. Nicolas, thanks to his opposition to the Jacobin administration, had lost his life during the Reign of Terror.

More than twenty years younger than her famous husband when she married, and renowned as an early feminist, Sophie de Condorcet was fluent in English and Italian, and already an accomplished translator of the works of Thomas Paine and Adam Smith. Her salon regularly attracted the leading figures of the enlightenment.

Unlike so many of her fellow *salonnières*, however, Madame de Condorcet's salons always included other women, including the infamous Madame de Staël, an opponent of Napoleon. De Staël would make a deep impression upon young Sophia, but they would never become more than casual acquaintances. Her relationship with the Condorcets, on the other hand, became quickly intimate, most especially with Sophie's daughter, Eliza, a delightful, intelligent, and animated eleven-year-old who had lost her father at the age of five.

Sophie de Condorcet, like Margaret Mount Cashel, was similarly possessed of extravagant political notions. A century before women would be given the vote and a full five years before slavery would be outlawed in Britain, she and her husband had been championing such radical ideas as a liberal economy, free and equal public education, and equal rights for women and people of all races. When she finally left Paris to return to London, Sophia Parnell took with her more than just memories. She took with her a newfound self-confidence and a head full of 'extravagant' notions.

Following her return to London, Sophia decided to remain on in the townhouse at 22 Eaton Square, where she proceeded to live alone on the fortune of £600 a year that her father had provided for her in his will. To understand the exclusivity of this address, it is worth noting that a single flat in the same house was advertised for sale in 2018 at an asking price of £12 million. And yet, despite the enormous financial incentives, there were no suitors, until at length George Evans, a young barrister from Portrane in north County Dublin, began to tip his hat in her direction.

They made for an unlikely couple: George, cautious and unassuming; and Sophia, an opinionated intellectual from a family known for oddities. Her eldest brother, John Augustus, was born a 'deaf and dumb imbecile' and housed in a walled garden for most of his life. Henry, who inherited the baronetcy at John Augustus' expense, suffered most of his life from depression, and Thomas was cursed with a form of religious mania that led him to devote his life to the search for 'infallible answers' in the random arrangement of biblical texts.

Though George Evans was a wealthy young man, he was not as wealthy as Sophia. Educated in Dublin rather than at Eton and Cambridge, where Sophia's brothers had been educated, he had entered Trinity College in 1788 as a *Socius Comitatus* or 'Gentleman Commoner'. Generous, well-liked, and liberal in his personal philosophy, he moved in the same literary circles as Sophia's brother William.

At the beginning of his relationship with Sophia, George appears to have had little interest in politics beyond its effect on his legal work, his family's estates, and the hospitality he was obliged to offer the more dangerous acquaintances of his father. Not even the visit of Robert Emmet, who dined with him at Portrane House in October 1802, could persuade George to offer support to another rebellion.

With his entire family dependent upon the income from the estates he now managed on behalf of his exiled father, George refused point-blank to get involved in anything that could jeopardise their collective futures. In 1798, his father, Hampden Evans, had only escaped the hangman's noose by the skin of his teeth. George was not about to make the same mistake.

Less than a year later, Robert Emmet was hung and beheaded on Dublin's Thomas Street. Such was the fear of being tainted by association, that not a single person came forward to claim his remains. George had been proved prudent in his caution but, that having been said, he was not without political opinions or beyond giving aid or support to non-violent campaigns.

In the year following Emmet's execution, Lord King approached William Parnell to discuss his intention to move a bill to abolish what remained of the penal laws. Advised by the prominent Whig statesman Charles Fox, that the necessary majority would be difficult to achieve unless a petition for relief was first received from the Catholics, the pair undertook to see to it that such a petition would be forthcoming.

On his return to Dublin, William went straight to Portrane to call on George Evans, who took him to see his friend, James Ryan, a wealthy Catholic merchant. Together they persuaded Ryan to canvas other influential Catholics, but neither was prepared to go further than that. It was a small step into the world of politics for George, but politics was the realm of the Parnells and the world in which his future wife had been raised. It was never going to be his last foray.

On Wednesday, 31 August 1805, the marriage settlements having been signed, thirty-four-year-old George Evans of Portrane married twenty-five-year-old Sophia Parnell of Avondale in County Wicklow, in one of the rare occasions in her adult life that Sophia, a 'deist of the old school', would see fit to visit a church. The ceremony took place at Marylebone in the City of Westminster, close to Sophia's townhouse in Belgravia, from where she departed for her new life in Portrane.

Portrane c.1844. Mount Evans in background top right.

Her new home was a substantial south-facing Georgian house that looked out over expansive lawns to Howth Head and the Wicklow mountains. A 'spacious' building that lay at the centre of a 420-acre demesne, it was drab and isolated compared to her house in Belgravia but in time she would grow to love the place and to mould it to her own tastes.

Having experienced the intellectual freedom of the French salons where wealthy educated women steered a course of their own charting, scorned 'delicate' conversation, and debated freely with men on matters of science, politics, economics, and the arts, the new Mrs. Evans chaffed at societal restrictions in Ireland. Described variously as *'une maitress femme'* and a 'resolute character' with the 'face of a lioness', she had entered, upon her marriage, into a cosy coterie of idealistic artists that was far removed from the groups of political strategists and pragmatists that had once congregated at her father's table.

Of her brothers, only Henry was now actively involved in politics, but he lived in London – too distant for regular contact or stimulating debate. Her younger brother, William, lived closer to home at the family estate in Avondale, but William was far more interested in expressing his views on paper than in any representative assembly. Like her new husband, her younger brother had always felt more at home in the company writers and poets than in the combative arena of professional politics.

A few months after the wedding, the poet, Mary Blanchford Tighe, composed a poem that poked fun at Sophia's new husband and eulogised the intellectually competitive nature of the artistic gatherings into which Sophia now found herself thrust. Within the lines of her *Letter from Mrs Acton to her Nephew Mr. Evans,* George's maternal aunt, Sidney Acton, warns her nephew to be prepared to deliver an entertaining and cultured performance if he planned to spend Christmas with the Tighes at Rosanna where, the poem asserts, one could hear fifteen languages spoken at table, the servants speak Latin and Greek, the ladies read Arabic and serve tea in Chinese, and the company enjoy food prepared to display the principles of chemistry, geometry, and trigonometry. At Rosanna, allegedly, everyone was 'a poetical genius.'

Sophia, however, was no artist. Her interests lay more in science, politics, and philosophy, than in literature. But an invitation had been issued, and if George was going to spend Christmas at Rosanna, then Sophia would be expected to accompany him. There, amongst the leisured ladies, there would at least be the prospect of some scandalous tittle-tattle to which she could add her tuppence worth, she being well-acquainted with one of the parties involved, and her new husband equally so with the other.

Shortly after Sophia and William left Paris, their close friend, Margaret Mount Cashel, began an illicit relationship with George Tighe, brother of the aforementioned poet Mary Tighe. The affair having been discovered, Stephen Mount Cashel had taken possession of his sons, abandoned his wife in Germany, and left her to flee with George Tighe to Italy.

In love for the first time in her life, Margaret had relinquished all trappings of social respectability, renamed herself Mrs. Mason (after the governess in Wollstonecraft's children's book *Original Stories from Real Life*), and plunged headlong into a life of poverty with the only man she would ever truly love. To some of her class she appeared heroic; to the remainder, she cut a somewhat ridiculous figure. One could hardly visit Rosanna that Christmas and not expect the matter to be discussed.

The unconventional couple had since settled in Jena, where the tall and muscular Margaret had begun to crossdress as a man in order to study medicine at the local university. She had also turned her hand to writing children's fiction and her *Stories of Old Daniel* would be published by William Godwin

(Mary Wollstonecraft's widower) in 1808. Some years later the infamous couple would move to Pisa, where Margaret would attend the University of Pisa and give birth to two daughters, Laurette and Nerina. Sophia, by way of contrast, would settle down to a conventional married life and would remain childless. They had both changed since Paris, and in drastically different ways.

Sophia almost returned to Paris in August of 1809. George's younger sister, Mary, who was still living with her parents on the Boulevard des Invalides, had been taken seriously ill and the family were fearing for her life. Mary had fallen in love with a frequent visitor to the family home, a surgeon by the name of William Lawless. Exiled along with her father, Hampden Evans, for the part they played in the 1798 rebellion, Lawless was currently serving in an Irish regiment of the French army. So well had Mary Evans concealed her infatuation that neither Lawless nor the Evans family had suspected it, until, that is, rumours of his disappearance at the Siege of Flushing reached Paris.

Poor Mary all but died of grief and not even the ministering of Wolfe Tone's widow could console her. Her health gradually recovered when Lawless was discovered to have survived and, upon his return, Hampden Evans quickly acquainted him with his daughter's feelings. A speedy marriage was arranged, two funerals were averted, and Sophia remained in Portrane, though she still maintained her connections to the city through her correspondence with Sophie de Condorcet and her daughter Eliza.

Little Eliza! How the years had flown! She was twenty years-of-age now, and married, with two baby boys, Arthur and Daniel. She had even followed in her mother's footsteps, by marrying, at the tender age of seventeen, a certain Arthur O'Connor, a man twenty-seven years her senior. Arthur, too, had been a veteran of 1798 and a fellow prisoner of Hampden Evans. Like

Hampden, he too had been spared execution with a last-minute reprieve and forced into exile. Arthurs' brother, Roger, was also a close friend of Sophia's husband, George Evans.

Sophie and Eliza were never short of things to write about and ever since that unusual wedding, in which the groom was almost exactly the same age as the mother of the bride, the newlyweds had been increasingly in contact with Sophia and George on account of Arthur's desire to liquidate his assets in Ireland and purchase the Chateau de Bignon – a 100-acre estate about seventy miles southeast of Paris. Arthur needed help. His landed property in Ireland had been put under the management of his brother, Roger, who treated it as his own and was reluctant to see it sold. Desperate for funds and forbidden from returning, Arthur asked George to intervene.

George did his best, but was constantly frustrated by Roger's stalling tactics and, after several years trying, and failing, to persuade Roger to act honourably, Arthur was left with little choice but to ask George to institute legal proceedings on his behalf. These proceedings, too, dragged on, and in an attempt to speed things up, Arthur finally decided to send twenty-five-year-old Eliza to Dublin to plead with Roger.

And so it was that, in 1815, Eliza and Sophia were finally reunited. It was, alas, to prove a short and unproductive visit. Roger knew that Eliza's visa was limited and found excuse after excuse to avoid meeting her. By the time she left Ireland, she had enjoyed no more success in her attempts at friendly arbitration than George Evans, who was now left with little option but to have Roger arrested and jailed. Thanks to George's help, Arthur finally managed to recover some small part of what remained of his inheritance. He had lost a brother, but gained a close and loyal friend.

In 1817, Sophia's brother, William, then serving as the

Deputy Lieutenant of Co. Wicklow, finally allowed himself to be persuaded to follow in the family tradition and enter Parliament as MP for Wicklow. Considering himself something of an outsider, he opted to act as an independent in opposition. As a member of the Irish Board of Education, William had translated the sermons Massillon and Bourdaloue for use in Irish country schools and dedicated his novel *The Priest of Rahery* to 'the Catholic priesthood of Ireland'. His liberal agenda promised a long career in parliament.

As for Sophia's husband, George, he had, until now, more or less maintained a low political profile. All of that changed, however, on 16 August 1819, when cavalry charged a crowd of 60,000 protestors gathered at St. Peter's Field in Manchester to demand the reform of a system of parliamentary representation that gave only 2% of the population a vote. This pro-democracy and anti-poverty gathering had been provoked by both the famine and the chronic unemployment that had followed the end of the Napoleonic Wars and, most especially, by the introduction of the Corn Laws, a body of legislation that had effectively led to bread becoming a luxury foodstuff. It was to have been addressed by the radical orator Henry Hunt.

An estimated 18 people, including four women and a child, died from sabre cuts and trampling, and almost 700 men, women, and children, were seriously maimed and injured. News of the atrocity so outraged George Evans that he made a public donation of fifty pounds to the appeal for funds to aid the victims and prompt an inquiry into what had become popularly known as the Peterloo Massacre.

Fifty pounds was an enormous sum in those days, and news of George's donation was carried in both the Irish and British press. Having well and truly nailed his colours to a liberal mast it appeared to all and sundry that George and his brother-in-law, William

Parnell were about to join forces in the fight against poverty and the campaign for universal suffrage. But it was not to be. On 2 January 1821, William Parnell caught a bad cold, developed a fever, and died. He was just forty-four years of age. At the time of his death, he had been actively sponsoring legislation to redeem the plight of the Irish poor.

On 15 February, an individual signing himself as 'C' wrote to the *Freeman's Journal* to eulogise William Parnell as a man who, 'not content to linger out his days in inactive and unprofitable sympathy' had set out to improve the standard of living and education of poor Catholics.

George Tighe and Margaret Mount Cashel had by this time been joined in Pisa by the poet Percy Shelley and his wife Mary (daughter of Mary Wollstonecraft and already the author of *Frankenstein*). Margaret felt a maternal bond with the young Mary Shelley and helped her to set up her household, find lodgings and hire servants. She also gave illness-prone and hypochondriacal Percy, the benefit of her medical training, helped Mary with the new baby, and broke up the couple's dysfunctional love triangle with Mary's stepsister Claire. The Tighes also introduced the Shelleys to a new intellectual circle, inspiring them, as Margaret had once inspired young Sophia Parnell, with a sense of youthful radicalism.

Given William Parnell's close friendship with Mary Tighe and Sophia's with Margaret Mount Cashel, it would be almost inconceivable to imagine that this radical couple's unconventional life in Italy was not commonly discussed at Portrane House. Sophia, in particular, could not have been left untouched by the intellectual freedom her old friend Margaret now appeared to enjoy.

Unable to pursue a political career of her own in this era before women's suffrage, Sophia had, prior to William's death, been content to busy herself improving Portrane Demesne and expressing her political beliefs through charitable donations and whatever influence she could exert upon her husband and brothers. Her interest in marine science had also led her to build a unique collection of Irish seashells and to entertain members of the Geological Society of Dublin who would come to Portrane to study the cliffs. To feed her insatiable interest in atheist writers such as Hume, Gibbon, Voltaire, and the *Encyclopédistes* she had also established a fine library at Portrane House, a library that was to be a considerable comfort to her in her old age.

But it was never enough. Sophia was very much an intellectual of the Enlightenment. Unlike Madame de Staël, however, whom she admired immensely, Sophia was no writer. She had little to say that hadn't been better expressed by someone else. What she did have, in spades, was the steely conviction and the necessary wealth to indulge her passions.

In the year following her brother's death, word reached Sophia of the death of her old friend and mentor, Sophie de Condorcet, and of the birth of Eliza's third child, a boy she had chosen to name for the man who had helped her husband regain his estates, George Evans. With Eliza determined to take up where her mother had left off and publish what remained of her father's writings, Sophia appears to have decided to take up where William had left off with regard to the education of the poor. No longer willing to spend her own energies in *inactive and unprofitable sympathy*, she determined to make a difference, even if it had, occasionally, to be through the proxy of her husband.

Sophia Parnell was no political *ingénue*, but the daughter of one of the most astute political operators of his day. Despite his liberal leanings and his wife's ambition, however, it was to be January of 1824 before George took his first tentative steps into the political arena. At a Vestry meeting at the Protestant church in

Donabate, he proposed and saw passed, two motions recommending the abolition of tithes, on the basis that:

'... in many Parishes the Protestant Clergyman is exclusively supported by the tithe of the Catholic Farmer, and the Tithe of the potato garden of the Cottier. We entertained hopes that the many would have been heavily taxed to support the religious opinions of the few'.

It was a small move, and very much at a local level, but the news still made the national newspapers. As a liberal and fair-minded landlord and lawyer who was known to be totally opposed to the Tories, it was only a matter of time before someone would ask George Evans to stand for parliament.

In November of 1825, Sophia finally returned to Paris. George's sister Mary, now residing on the fashionable Rue de Colombier, had recently been widowed. Her husband, William Lawless, had died the previous Christmas at the age of 52.

On this occasion, there was to be no reprieve from her grief and George had could only put off visiting his sister for so long. Grateful for the opportunity, after so many years, to renew her friendship with Eliza de Condorcet, Sophia decided to travel with him. It would allow her an opportunity to see Sophia's son, George, now be three years of age.

Her return to Paris, however, was not without a dash of the clandestine. About her person, she carried a personal letter from the famous novelist Lady Morgan, author of *The Wild Irish Girl*, to Elizabeth 'Betsy' Patterson, ex-wife of Napoleon's younger brother, Jérôme. Morgan, a frequent guest at Portrane House and a correspondent of Betsy's for many years, was reluctant to entrust her letter to the postal service.

An Irish-American socialite famous for her risqué dress sense, Elizabeth 'Betsy' Patterson had married Jerome Bonaparte in Baltimore on Christmas Eve 1803. Napoleon, who disapproved of the marriage, demanded that it be annulled and that his brother return to France without her. Jérôme, however, ignored Napoleon, and in the autumn of 1804, attempted to travel with pregnant Elizabeth to his brother's coronation, only to find that Elizabeth had been

Elizabeth Patterson Bonaparte

banned from setting foot anywhere in continental Europe.

Jérôme set off for Italy to reason with his brother and Elizabeth never saw him again. Three years later, despite still being married to Elizabeth, he married the German princess, Catharina of Württemberg. Elizabeth fled to London where she gave birth to a son, Jerome Napoleon Bonaparte, before returning to Baltimore to live with her Donegal-born father.

Following Napoleon's defeat at Waterloo, Elizabeth returned to Paris to flaunt her Napoleonic connections. Newly divorced, but not remarried, she was well-received in exclusive circles but found herself constantly watched and her movements carefully monitored. She longed for letters from friends that had not been intercepted by the police. Lady Morgan, suspecting that this might well be the case, had therefore entrusted hers to Sophia Evans.

Elizabeth Patterson knew everyone of consequence in continental Europe and her letters to her friends frequently contained gossip of the great names of politics, literature, and the royal courts. Not since her youthful meeting with Madame de Staël had Sophia met such a woman, and the visit gave fresh impetus to her social aspirations and invigorated her ambitions for her husband. For all of her liberal tendencies, Sophia Evans was still very much a child of her class.

George and Sophia would never be blessed with children of their own and, with no children to support, Sophia decided to dedicate at least some of her time and personal wealth to the children of her less fortunate neighbours. The education of the poor, so long a passion of her late brother William, would now be hers.

Sophia had no sooner returned from Paris when her husband George was persuaded to serve on the committee of the *Education Society to Establish Free Schools for the Moral and Useful Instruction of the Poor.*

Shortly afterwards, in 1827, she and George founded and funded two public schools in Donabate. Though George and Sophia would each endow the school of their respective genders, the driving force behind the scheme, and the building of *both* schools, was widely known to be Sophia, who was also listed in Department of Education records as the schools' 'manager'.

These schools were established and run according to the Lancastrian system, in which an experienced teacher taught a select group of older children, who then taught the younger or weaker pupils in small groups. They were also, at least nominally, multi-denominational. There were, however, few Church of Ireland children living in the Donabate or Portrane area who would have required public schooling, and the teachers that Sophia employed were both Catholic. In all of this, Sophia remained faithful to the work of her late brother, William, whose ideals would subsequently be embodied in Ireland's fledgling system of primary education.

George and Sophia Evans were by now known to be passionate and vocal supporters of universal suffrage, Catholic emancipation, and the abolition of tithes. The creation of the schools in Donabate, therefore, was bound not just to reflect their politics, but to be noticed. In 1827, in her book *The O'Briens and the O'Flahertys*, Lady Morgan described George Evans as:

'a good landlord, a liberal politician, and one of the few who still hold by the country which gave them birth and subsistence, and reflect back upon it the high benefits of enlightened and well-directed patriotism.'

In December of that same year, Sophia Evans received even greater praise, this time from Daniel O'Connell, who read an excerpt from a letter that he had recently received from the parish priest of Donabate to a meeting of his newly formed Catholic

Association:

'There is an extensive school for females in Portrane, carried on with liberality and munificence truly characteristic and worthy of the amiable and benevolent lady who has established, and supports it solely at her own expense, unconnected with any other Education Society or Association whatsoever. The mistress is a Catholic, has an annual salary of twenty guineas, house and coals free, with other perquisites. No book, no publication is introduced without the approbation of the Parish Priest.

There are from fifty to a hundred children, all Catholics, instructed in reading, writing, arithmetic, and in all kind of needlework, provided with stationery, and all, this year, handsomely clothed at this Protestant Lady's expense. It is almost impossible to conceive the vast utility, the manifold good resulting from this liberal school. I need scarcely say that this humane and distinguished lady, to whom the parents and the rising generation of this parish owe so much, is Mrs. Evans, wife of George Evans Esq., and sister to Sir Henry Parnell.

The boys' school is not as yet carried on with any kind of system, as we have had the building of a new one in contemplation. The erection of this school-house, forty feet long by twenty wide, Mr. Evans has kindly and generously taken upon himself, at his sole expense, and has given a commodious site, together with a portion of land, rent free, as an equivalent for the free tuition of the poor Catholic children of this parish....'

O'Connell, having read the Rev. Murray's letter, moved that Murray be requested to discover an appropriate means of expressing the 'heartfelt gratitude and admiration of the Catholic Association' to Mrs. Evans. He did not acknowledge George Evans, of which more anon.

Having dipped his toes in the arena of public service

and found that he quite liked it, George Evans accepted another appointment, three years later, as High Sheriff of County Dublin, his first real taste of political power. As the Sovereign's legal representative George became responsible for judicial, ceremonial, and administrative duties and the execution High Court writs. The appointment, shared on an annual basis amongst the landed gentry, temporarily satisfied his wife's hankering for a return to the political milieu of her childhood. But Dublin wasn't London, or Paris for that matter, reminders of which kept raising their heads.

In October of 1829, having doubtlessly heard of George's promotion, the Condorcet-O'Connors came calling once again. Their eldest son, Arthur junior, had died that year at the age of twenty, and their second son, Daniel, having just turned nineteen, was now the legal heir. In order to 'inherit his real property in Ireland', however, Daniel needed to be naturalised as an Irishman. George agreed to take on his case and wrote a personal letter to Francis Levenson Gower, the Chief Secretary, on their behalf.

George's public profile was slowly rising and by 1830 he was to be found acting as the foreman of the Grand Jury of County Dublin and protesting to the Chief Secretary on such diverse matters as the granting of planning permission for houses without any space for accumulated refuse, and the exorbitant fees being imposed on the County by surgeons in respect of their attendance at coroner's inquests. Slowly, but surely, his legal career was being left behind and George Evans was becoming a politician. Daniel O'Connor's naturalisation would be one of the last legal cases he would take.

Following the passing of the Act of Emancipation, the Irish Catholic politician, Daniel O'Connell, set his sights on repealing the Acts of Union and returning Ireland to a position of legislative independence under the British Crown, i.e. with an Irish parliament sitting in Dublin and with full Catholic involvement. The *Repeal Association* that O'Connell founded proceeded to select candidates to be put forward at the United Kingdom general election of 1832, but in north County Dublin they found themselves faced with a totally unexpected challenge.

Despite the fact that George was due to take his master's examinations in law just a month before the polls opened, and the fact that his nephew William Lawless had recently been seriously injured in a shooting accident at Portrane – an accident that had caused George to suffer a 'bilious attack' – George proceeded to declare his candidacy. His manifesto was carried in the pages of *The Freeman's Journal*:

'Having neither personal interests to advance, nor any object of ambition to attain, my future actions will continue to be guided, as my past have been, solely by what I honestly conceive to be for the advantage of my native country. My watch words of Parliamentary duty will be Education, Economy, and equal rights to all.'

Acting, it was said, like a modern-day Madame Roland, Sophia developed a network of political and journalistic contacts, drew upon her own intelligence and family experience, and helped to manage her husband's campaign. His election agent even began to lobby the new Chief Secretary, Edward Smith Stanley, on the inconvenience to freeholders in north County Dublin having to travel to Kilmainham to register as voters. For a first-time candidate, and an independent to boot, George's campaign was run with extraordinary professionalism and attention to detail.

There was, however, a fly in the ointment. George was not totally opposed to the repeal of the Act of Union, but there were many local landlords who were, not least his neighbour Charles Cobbe of Newbridge Demesne. As voting at this time still had to be made in public, a tenant who voted against the wishes of his landlord could well expect to feel the consequences and George was only too well aware that he needed the votes of his neighbours' tenants to be elected. He decided, therefore, to sit on the fence and claim that, while he was not opposed to repeal of the Union, he nevertheless felt that the country was 'not at present sufficiently united to hazard a separation from England'. His duplicity infuriated O'Connell and the spat became intensely personal.

Despite O'Connell's campaign of intimidation, George, with his wife's encouragement, held his nerve and, much to O'Connell's annoyance, succeeded in getting himself elected. Of all his supporters, there was none more pleased than his wife. Observing that delight, Lady Morgan would famously comment that Sophia Evans was 'a first-rate woman, but, perhaps, too ambitious about her husband's parliamentary career.'

George's duplicity may have helped to get him elected, but the storm of criticism it brought down upon him did not disappear once the election was over. In January of 1834, at a public meeting in Rathmines, O'Connell once again attempted to expose George's stance to public ridicule:

'I once heard of a woman who, seeing a man executed for forgery, put on a resolution that her eleven sons should never learn to write. Now, it would be well for George Evans if he had not been taught writing, and his mother was not an honest woman to allow him to be instructed. He says he will contribute to the abolition of tithes. So far so well. It is putting his best leg foremost: but I fear he is ham-strung in the other. There is a large class standing up for the continuance of the tithe system – the men who, by peculation and robbery, fatten on the miseries of the poor – and we are not as divided on Repeal as we are on the abolition of tithes.

George Evans gives the same reason for opposing the

Repeal, and aiding in the abolition of tithes. There's a fellow for you! I think the next time you are choosing a Representative you will discard him. (Cheers) As many as are of that opinion will say 'aye' – the contrary will say 'no' (Loud cries of 'aye.')

The ayes have it – carried unanimously. (Cheers and laughter). I verily believe that there never was more folly than in the letter of George Evans; and it is a deplorable and sad condition for the metropolitain county to be represented by one of the Cloncurry clique...'

George disliked O'Connell intensely. He considered him autocratic, arrogant, and more than a little presumptuous in claiming to speak for *all* sections of Irish society. He particularly disliked O'Connell's attitude towards the landed gentry. Stung by the increasingly personal nature of the attacks, he accused O'Connell of trying to silence 'men of property and education'.

O'Connell, of course, was having none of it. He knew his public and was never afraid to play to the gallery. He dismissed George as nothing more than a 'landlord and a Whig'. Indeed, George could hardly have expected less from a man who had taken to signing his letters as 'Daniel O'Connell, Liberator of Ireland', and who at one time or another had fallen out with almost every other nationalist politician with whom he had disagreed.

Truth be told, the Evans family had always been much more than liberal-minded landlords. George's father, Hampden, had been a member of the Society of United Irishmen and a friend of such revolutionary figures as Lord Edward Fitzgerald, Thomas Addis Emmet, Hamilton Rowan, and Wolfe Tone, the latter of whom, local tradition has long held, visited Evans in Portrane in February of 1796 on the eve of his departure to Paris to seek French support for a rebellion.

Like many other Protestants inspired by the French and American revolutions, Hampden Evans had been quick to volunteer when the Society evolved into a paramilitary organisation and served as a colonel in the Rotunda Division during the rebellion of 1798. The rebellion, alas, failed miserably. A French army sent to assist the revolution was overwhelmed by British forces and Hampden was betrayed by a certain Thomas Boyle, who implicated him, along with a Father Teeling of Donabate, in a plot to assassinate Lord Carhampton, the commander-in-chief of the British army in Ireland.

Following his arrest and imprisonment, Hampden had been facing execution when he was granted a last-minute reprieve on condition that he went into voluntary exile in Germany. Later, allowed to move to Paris on grounds of ill-health, he had set up home with his wife and children in a house on the Boulevard des Invalides, where he continued to entertain many of his old colleagues, including the Wicklow rebel, Myles Byrne. Such revolutionary connections, however, cut little ice with O'Connell, a staunch pacifist.

Despite his father's nationalist instincts, George Evans had somehow managed to avoid getting caught up in the rebellion of 1798 and had been allowed to remain in Ireland to take care of the family estates, at least until 1811, when Hampden was finally permitted to return. George would not inherit the estate outright until Hampden's death in 1820, but from that point onwards he would always choose to express his patriotism and responsibilities as a landlord in an understated and pragmatic manner. George's greatest fear was losing his home. Unlike his father, he was not, and would never be, a risk-taker.

George's personal brand of nationalism would always be weighted more heavily towards some form of devolved government than outright separation. There were economic benefits to the country that flowed from being part of the British Empire that he was reluctant to see lost. George, and indeed Sophia, also enjoyed London society and the trappings of a parliamentary seat. But for all that, George Evans still considered himself an Irishman and his loyalty remained first and foremost to his constituents.

Sydney Owenson (Lady Morgan)

At the time of O'Connell's rebuke, George and Sophia were financing the education of local Catholic children and pensioning the poorest of the elderly population of Ballisk to prevent them from falling into destitution. O'Connell was well aware of this, and of other acts of atypical liberalism, and yet he still chose to persist with personal attacks against George.

Perhaps too thin-skinned to be an effective politician, George was deeply wounded. 'I belong to no party,' he famously hit back, 'I have no object in view but the happiness and prosperity of Ireland'. Indeed, he would sooner, or so he claimed, 'be doomed to perpetual exile than submit to such a tyranny'. In her memoirs, Lady Morgan sympathetically recalled his plight, describing him as 'the butt and victim of all O'Connell's hatred, malice, and calumny, because he will not crawl after him and resists his appeal.' Such was the nature of politics, that just five months after their very public spat, Evans and O'Connell managed to put the matter of Repeal behind them and jointly form the Anti-Tory Association in Dublin. O'Connell's campaign of public vilification, however, was never entirely forgotten, at least not by Sophia.

The spat with O'Connell notwithstanding, the years following George's election saw Sophia return to a social circle she had not experienced since her tour of France in 1802 as she travelled on an annual basis with George to London for 'The Season', which took place between the months of February and July to coincide with the sitting of parliament.

It was during these trips that Sophia and George became good friends of the family of Charles Darwin, the famous naturalist. If George had been fascinated by Darwin's voyage, his wife had been painfully envious of it. This was exactly the type of adventure she would have loved to have undertaken herself, had she not been born female. Sophia would become good friends with Catherine and Caroline Darwin, and George likewise with Erasmus, Charles' older brother, and would be frequently mentioned in letters received by Charles aboard *The Beagle*:

'We heard from Erasmus who seems very happy & seemingly leading a dissipated life for him. Mr. & Mrs. Evans of Portrane are in London & he sees a good deal of them. Mr. Evans is in Parliament for the County of Dublin.'

Caroline Darwin, May 1st 1833.

*'Do you remember the Evans of Portrane in Ireland?
Mr. Evans is Member for the County of Dublin, so they
are in London, and are very nice friends for us. We are
going with them and a large party down to Richmond
by steam on Saturday, dine there, and return in the
Evening. – Mrs. Evans enquired very much after you,
and said that she could not conceive any thing she
should enjoy more than your Voyage.'*

Catherine Darwin, May 29th 1833.

*'We staid at Osmaston about 10 days & when we
came back Erasmus came home and has been with us
ever since. I think he will go no expedition this summer
but return to London when he leaves us. Mrs. Evans of
Portrane wanted to persuade him to go with her into
Scotland, & I believe he would if he had not discovered
there were to be some young ladies of the party who he
disliked.'*

Caroline Darwin, September 1st 1833.

In October of 1836, the Beagle returned to England
and Charles Darwin returned for a while to Cambridge
before settling in London, where his older brother
Erasmus, was living. During this time his sister,
Catherine, pleaded with him to meet with George
Evans, who had for so long wished to meet him:

*'I want you to see the Evans sometime; they are at
Ibbotson's Hotel and Mr. Evans talked much about you,
and how much he wished to see you; he had heard of
you from Mrs. Warren, who had heard again from Mr.
Lyell. – Pray write us an account of your London trip,
when you return to the quiet of Cambridge.'*

Catherine Darwin, February 16th 1837.

And then there was the not inconsequential matter

of royalty. As part of the 'London Season' Sophia would make occasional visits to St. James' Palace for those drawing room occasions at which women of the nobility and gentry would be presented to the Queen. She was presented to Queen Adelaide in May, 1834 by the Countess of Rosse, and later, in October, 1836, she herself would present a Mrs J. Wood. Two years later again, in April, 1838, Sophia was presented to Queen Victoria by Hester Catherine Browne, the Marchioness of Sligo. Such grand occasions intensified Sophia's ambition for her husband. Her father and eldest brother had been knighted and had achieved high office. Why not George?

Alas, it was not to be. Despite the fact O'Connell would make funds from the Repeal Association available to George for the general election of 1841, George would ultimately lose his seat to the Tory candidate. It probably did not help his broader appeal that in a letter to the *Freeman's Journal* – on July 12th of all dates – he had described Queen Victoria as 'The Queen of Ireland'. That last-minute appeal to the Tory heartland, however, failed to convince and an increasingly polarised electorate struggled to understand what George actually stood for.

Subsequently appointed to the Privy Council of Ireland and the Central Loan Fund Board of Ireland, George now found himself on the fringes of political life. But whatever disappointment Sophia may have endured upon her husband's demotion, it was to quickly pale against the series of tragic events that were soon to follow.

On the morning of 8 June 1842, Sophia's brother, Sir Henry Parnell, while in residence at his Chelsea townhouse, failed to come down to breakfast following a visit from his hairdresser. A couple of minutes after midday, afraid that something was amiss, his valet, Isaac Manning, went up his bedroom to enquire on him. He found him hanging from his bedpost by his cravat in what appeared to be an act of suicide. Henry had been suffering from severe depression for quite some time and the fear of suicide had been so great that his eldest son had been advised to lock up his father's razors and remove the bell rope from his room.

Sophia had scarcely returned from her brother's funeral when, just 24 days later, she fell prey to fresh misfortune. In the early hours of Saturday, 2 July 1842, her husband was taken ill. Gripped, perhaps, by a portent of impending doom, George had gone for a long walk the previous day, surveying all that he owned and all that he would leave behind. Between two and three of the following morning, he became so alarmingly ill that his wife, convinced that he had been struck down with cholera, sent a carriage to fetch his physician, Dr. O'Grady, from his home near Malahide.

O'Grady remained with George until 3pm the following day, at which point the patient was looking so much better that the good doctor left his bedside. O'Grady had no sooner departed, however, when George called for a drink and, having taken a sip from the cup, fell backwards and died. His death was attributed to 'an attack of flying gout to the heart'.

The following Monday, the Freemans Journal printed a brief obituary:

'The right hon. gentleman was a Whig of the most popular school, and his influence in the county of Dublin, which, both on account of his station and property, as well as character, was considerable, and always exercised in furtherance of the cause of reform. He was a good and indulgent landlord, and as far as a Whig might be, a good Irishman. He was thoroughly and determinedly opposed to Toryism; he was a good and indulgent landlord, and fully recognised the rights of freedom of election...'

At fifty-nine years of age, Sophia could share her double grief only with her mother-in-law, Margaret Evans, now in her nineties. Having lived vicariously through the lives and works of her husband and brothers, Sophia was utterly bereft. By tradition, she had two years of official mourning to mull over her future: two years in which widows were expected to abstain from entering society; two long years in which she would have to content herself with the visits of sympathetic neighbours, nephews, and nieces. But her energy had neither waned nor diminished. She didn't need sympathy; what she needed, was a project.

As the bewigged and green-suited 'Liberator' travelled the country, invoking all manner of Celtic symbolism and holding monster meetings at historic sites, it must have seemed to Sophia as if George's discreet patriotism and charitable works, not to mention his family's role in the 1798 rebellion, were all about to be erased from history by a growing tide of Catholic nationalism that seemed hell-bent on appropriating the country's revolutionary history as a solely Catholic tradition.

Something had to be done. While others of their class had vacillated, her husband's family had put their lives on the line in the quest for Irish freedom. While others of their class had sat in *inactive and unprofitable sympathy*, George Evans, like her brother William, had put himself forward for election and had fought for electoral and legislative equality. People needed to be reminded of all that, now more than ever. But what was to be done? How could people be *made* to remember? A monument of some sort was called for; a monument that would be visible for miles; a monument that spoke to both George's goodness *and* his patriotism.

Just two years had passed since the founding of the Archaeological Society in Dublin and interest in Ireland's 'Celtic' heritage was becoming increasingly fashionable, especially amongst the landed gentry. A revival of interest was similarly underway in Ireland's round towers, triggered in no small part by the decision of the Royal Irish Academy to hold an essay competition on their purpose and origins. With George Petrie, the eventual winner, promoting his theories through the pages of the Dublin Penny Journal the towers had become the subject of much topical and public debate.

If a fit mode to mark her husband's passing was to be found, Sophia now judged, it would inevitably have to be in the shape of a monument. And if that monument was to make a lasting impact on the landscape, and on the denizens of a peninsula that George had worked so assiduously to represent, then it simply *had* to be a tower.

George had been buried with his father, Hampden Evans, within the roofless ruins of Saint Catherine's, the old Church of Ireland parish church in Portrane. The memorial tower that his wife now commissioned would be built on a hill that overlooked George's grave from the south. Designed by the architect George Millar, at the exorbitant cost of £1,240, it would be the first round tower to have been built on Irish soil since the Norman invasion.

Saint Catherine's Church, Portrane

Some expertise had obviously been called upon in the tower's design, for it made every effort to conform to historical proportions, the architect allegedly using as his model the round tower at St. Brigid's Cathedral in Kildare town. But Sophia wasn't content to simply build *a* tower, it had to be *George's* tower and so, at the same time as the tower was being constructed, she commissioned the sculptor Christopher Moore to make a marble bust of her husband complete with coat of arms and the following dedication:

'To the memory of George Evans M.P., an honest man, firm friend and true patriot. This monument, a revival of the ancient architecture of his country, is respectfully, affectionately and mournfully dedicated.'

Notice the deliberate selection of the third person possessive: *his* country. Notice also the qualifying adjective in *true* patriot. And, as if to underscore her late husband's nationalist credentials, she had the tower built close to the very spot where, according to local tradition, Wolfe Tone had bid farewell to Hampden Evans on his departure for France. Despite the ecclesiastical history of the ancient towers, the word *Christian* was never even alluded to. Her husband may have been Protestant, but Sophia herself had issues with organised religion.

Sophia Evans had never been a regular visitor to the small Anglican church in Donabate, attending only when compelled to do so by societal requirements or accompanying house guests who wished to attend. As a result, she was not on good terms with the local vicar who, on one occasion, even dared to 'read' her from the pulpit.

While attending a Sunday service with some house guests, a large dog, that may or may not have been her own, followed Sophia into the church and lay down at her feet. Sophia made no attempt to shoo the animal out and no one dared to approach her on the matter.

Bust of George Evans.
Image courtesy of John Evans-Pritchard.

During the service, the constant rapping of the dog's tail during his sermon so infuriated the venerable gentleman of the pulpit that he interrupted his reading to turn on Sophia Evans. 'Turn out that dog if you please!' he raged, 'it's extremely wrong to bring a dog into a church!' The entire affair so amused one young local woman that she made a note of it in her diaries. She never recorded what happened next. It was scandal enough for Frances Power Cobbe that Sophia Evans had had the temerity to enter the church with a dog.

That same year, the former Physician to the King, James Johnson, visited Portrane on his tour of Ireland and became quite excited about the 'Widow's Tower' that he discovered under construction at Portrane. He noted particularly how it had fallen to a lady of noble birth to:

'conceive the idea of a monument to the memory of her deceased lord, that would survive the Pyramids themselves, and transmit their joint names to the latest posterity – in the perfect model and dimensions of the ancient Irish Round Towers'.

Five thousand years hence, Johnson went on to speculate,

'... the Tower of Portrane will probably be the only surviving representative of that ancient family of Round Towers, whose origin and pedigree have puzzled the antiquarian literati for nearly a thousand years past.'

In her bold choice of a replica round tower to serve as a memorial for a Protestant MP, Sophia Evans had both reclaimed that part of her husband's heritage that so many had appeared determined to deny, and in the process had found herself setting in train a fashion for memorial towers that would endure long after her death.

The winters were cruel. There was no shortage of visitors to her well-appointed coastal mansion in summer, but hardly any relatives visited in winter. The darker months, however, were not altogether without their compensations.

One of the few comforts of her widowhood was the unlikely friendship Sophia had struck up with a young lady in her early twenties, the daughter of a former political adversary from up the road in Donabate. Three score years and change lay between Frances Power Cobbe and Sophia Evans, and political differences between Frances's father and Sophia's husband had long served to keep the two families at arm's length.

Following George's death, however, the Cobbles had reached out to Sophia in her grief and isolation, and she and Frances had quickly become, in Frances's words, 'pleasantly intimate'. This unlikely friendship was forged, initially at least, in a shared and fruitless opposition to the new Dublin to Drogheda railway line that was planned to run through the village of Donabate. Following the opening of the line, however, an agreement between the two families to share the annual cost of establishing a post office in the village more or less cemented the friendship.

Sophia and Frances had much in common. Both had grown up as the only daughter in a brood of brothers; both were voracious readers and largely self-educated; both were non-conformist in matters of religion and resentful of the privileges accorded by right to their male siblings. When Cambridge University finally opened its doors to women, in 1869, it would be largely on account of the restless campaigning of Frances Power Cobbe, who famously presented a paper to the Social Science Congress of 1862 titled *Female Education, and How It Would be Affected by University Examinations.*

For years previous to the birth of their friendship, Frances had deflected her parents' attempt to turn her into a young society lady. Truth be told, she was not an overly attractive young woman and she would always feel more at home in the woods than in the ballroom. She never made any great effort to make herself attractive to men and was vehemently opposed to the wearing of corsets and the female invalidism she believed them to cause. She would often joke about having been born into a body which 'however defective ... from the aesthetic point of view', had been so robust and healthy as to be a 'source of endless enjoyment'. The botanist, Joseph Dalton Hooker, in a letter to Charles Darwin, once referred to her as a 'disenchanting mountain of flesh'.

Frances Power Cobbe at 72.

Frances was also a lesbian – a fact she had yet to fully come to terms with in 1845 – but in Sophia Evans, she appears to have found the tolerance and understanding she could never fully enjoy at home; a fellow victim, perhaps, of the nods and winks of the local gossips.

One evening as Frances, who in later years would achieve fame as a suffragette and early animal rights campaigner, was travelling from Donabate by coach to seven o'clock dinner at the home of her 'very kind old friend', Mrs Evans, when she passed a field of potatoes. Observing the leafy display, she remarked to her companions on how splendid it was looking and predicted a bumper crop.

Three or four hours later, as she returned home in the dark, a dreadful smell wafted from the same field. 'Something has happened to those potatoes,' someone in her carriage exclaimed, 'they do not smell at all as they did when we passed them on our way out.' They were witnessing a pivotal moment in Irish history. The potato crop had been hit by blight and Ireland would soon be devastated by famine and disease. Over the coming years, a million people would lose their lives.

On 13 March 1846, ninety-five-year-old Margaret Evans, George's mother, died. Her death left Sophia, who had only just returned from London, alone in a large twelve-bedroom house with just her servants and her books for company. Financially too, she was in some difficulty. The cost of building the tower had taxed her severely and her generosity to her tenants during the famine was now taxing her even more. The estate needed careful management if she was not to face bankruptcy, but she had been fortunate. Seven years previous to the famine she had taken a chance on a young land steward by the name of William Kelly. It was to prove one of the best decisions of her life.

Approximately 75% of the potato crop was lost in Fingal in 1845, followed by an almost complete loss in

1846. As the tenant farmers of Ireland relied heavily on the potato for food, the result for most parts of the country had been famine and disease. Between the years 1841 and 1851, the surrounding agricultural areas saw their populations fall by 12-20%. On the Donabate-Portrane peninsula, however, it fell by 0.8%., i.e. from 1170 people in 1841, to 1160 in 1851.

This was in part due to Sophia Evans, who had been advancing loans to her tenants with little hope of ever being repaid. In 1846 these loans averaged out at approximately five weeks wages and were accompanied by 'gratuities' that she ordered be paid to her labourers for as long as food prices remained unreasonably high. When added to the cost of building her round tower, the effect on her finances proved so severe that she suddenly decided to apply to the National Education Board for a grant to help cover the cost of running the two local schools she had founded and for which enrolment had recently escalated.

For fifteen years Sophia had resisted making such an application, despite being perfectly entitled to do so, preferring to run the schools independent of outside interference. In her application for funding she was still, at the age of sixty-six, listed as the schools' manager. She was granted 100 school books and the salary for a teacher.

Another reason the famine was not felt more deeply in Portrane was the radical land management practices of Sophia's steward, William Kelly. Before the famine, Sophia had ordered the bogs surrounding her estate to be drained and reclaimed, providing much-needed work for local labourers and extra land for her tenants to grow alternative crops. When the famine struck, Kelly acted quickly. He stabled his machinery and reverted to manual labour, providing extra employment in the area. He even found work for the children of the labourers in the dibbling of seeds.

And it didn't stop there. During the famine, the most cost-effective means of providing food relief, it was quickly found, was to import cheap poor-quality maize or 'Indian meal' from Britain's Indian colonies. Daily survival rations were set at a pound of meal per day for adults, and half a pound of meal per day for children. The meal was generally ground and added to warm water.

Kelly, his attention having been drawn by Sophia to a recent newspaper article concerning the experiments of a Viennese baker with wheat and beetroot, began to experiment, mixing varying quantities of Indian meal with cheaper crops. The crop Kelly finally settled on was mangelwurzel, a type of beet grown primarily for livestock feed.

This plant had begun life in Germany as *mangold-wurzel*, literally 'root of the beet', but this was, apparently, misheard as *mangel-wurzel* or 'root of scarcity'. The latter translation made its way to France as *racine de disette* and, in the previous century, an English translation of a French work by the Abbé de Commerell had introduced this plant to the English-speaking world by the same name.

Drawn by the etymologically suspect nomenclature to the possible use of the plant for human consumption, Kelly had acted with the irresistible urge of the visionary and his bread proved so popular on the peninsula that within weeks it was in 'extensive use'. On 12 December 1846, he offered samples to the Practical Agricultural Association and seven days later to the Royal Dublin Society. Days later the national newspapers were carrying a description of the bread.

With the potatoes rotting in the fields and the wheat and oats that would normally go pay the landlord now being consumed by the tenants leaving them little profit to pay rents, this new type of bread eased the burden of tenant farmers by reducing their consumption of expensive wheat in favour of a cheaper crop.

Kelly also knew, from practical and experimental experience at Portrane, that better land management and a reduction in reliance on the potato could prevent the famine from recurring. He began, therefore, to campaign for change. On 8 December 1846, a paper by him was read to the weekly meeting of the new Farmers' Club or Practical Agricultural Society at Northumberland Buildings in Dublin and reported five days later in the *Leinster Express*. In this paper, Kelly advised as to the type of crops that should be grown during the current emergency and gave instructions on the most efficient way to grow them.

So successful were Evans and Kelly in mitigating the effects of the famine in their own locality that Kelly was invited by The Irish Farmers Association to share his methods with the country at large. His *Irish Small Farmer of 1847; Containing Ample Directions for the Cultivation of the Soil During the Present Crisis was published in January of 1847*, and was aimed at helping tenant farmers move away from their reliance on the potato and teaching them how to cultivate alternative crops and maximise their yield.

Kelly's book took a revolutionary and modern approach to subjects such as economy of labour and food resources; land reclamation and drainage; manure making and application; tillage and deepening of the soil; systems of crop rotation; crop management; the comparative merits of crops for cattle and people; calf rearing and cow feeding; dairy management; garden crops; beekeeping and cottage economy. It even dealt with hygiene and the recycling of human waste. Just four months later many of his ideas were being quoted in other publications and by other 'experts'. In their work together, Sophia Evans and William Kelly had placed Portrane at the heart of an agricultural revolution.

That September, a front page article in the *Irish Examiner* waxed lyrical on the work of Sophia Evans:

'Ballyphehane, if reclaimed,' the contributor stated, 'is capable of producing as good crops of every kind as

those grown on similar land by Mrs. Evans of Portrane, in the county Dublin. The name of Portrane is now associated with the history of the improved agriculture of Europe, aye, and America, too. Cannot government, or a public body with a suitable staff, do that which a widow lady did by the aid of one practical Irishman?'

Sophia and William's fame even spread as far as Canada where the Lower Canada Agricultural Society noted in its journal Sophia Evans' success in November of 1848 at the Royal Dublin Society, and her 'very large returns' of other crops:

'The same lady got the first prize for the yellow globe mangel, cultivated in the same way, and having the same produce. Both were sown in the second week of May. She also obtained the first prize for carrots, of which the produce was over 60 tons to the Irish acre: manure, 3cwt of guano to the acre; cultivation, beds in rows twelve inches apart, plants 5 inches apart – sown 2nd May. Crop tilled exclusively with the spade, and the report states "the crops on the head lands which would be waste if the plough was used, would remunerate for the entire labour employed."
The lady took four prizes (all that were offered) for very great crops of beans and peas, which is a very good estimate of what a lady can do in the way of farming, and against such competitors as the Duke of Leinster, the Earls of Claremont and Meath, and many others of high rank.'

In proving herself the equal of the great titled landowners, Sophia began to cultivate a notion of herself as a force in the world in her own right, and she was not afraid to make difficult choices to enhance it.

Ireland remained in the grips of a famine and Sophia's multiplicity of charitable labours notwithstanding (apart from her schools she was also supporting a women's refuge), by the spring of 1849 things had gotten so bad in north County Dublin that the tenant farmers of the district finally roused themselves from their fatalistic slumber. Following a public meeting in Swords, they became the first tenants in the country to attempt to 'bring the landlords to a sense of the altered state of things' by means of a campaign of public embarrassment.

In the hope of forcing their landlords into a fair abatement of rents, they published their plight and resolutions in the newspapers. The strategy proved moderately successful. Modest reductions were offered by many of the local landowners, but Sophia Evans broke ranks. Her exceptional generosity even merited special mention in the *London Express*:

'Mrs. Evans of Portrane, whose charities to the poor have been so constant and liberal during the distress, has made an abatement of 20 per cent to her tenantry.'

William Kelly's agricultural papers were so widely published during the famine that his influence on Irish agriculture may well be greater than anyone has ever realised. None of that would have been possible without the vision, support, and charity of Sophia Evans. The land and money, after all, were hers; Kelly's experiments and local rent reductions dependent upon her direction and permission.

Following her mother-in-law's death, Portrane House became little more than a summer residence to Sophia, where she would pass the time alone among her books and surrounded by her old servants. Despite her advanced age, however, she had lost little of her old energy and was still more than capable of throwing a party, not to mention engaging in practical jokes at the expense of her guests.

Sophia had never forgotten the powerful women she had met in France and loved to scandalise her more conservative dinner guests with the story of her first meeting with the ineffable Madame de Staël. On that memorable occasion, as the French ladies retired to the drawing room, they endeavoured to seat themselves apart from the infamous Madame in sheer terror while she glowered upon them in obvious disdain.

After a short while, De Staël, tiring of their delicate conversation and doe-eyed blandness, rose from her seat. Without bothering to seek the consent of the mistress of the house, she rang the bell and ordered a footman to instruct the gentlemen, who would have been just settling down to their cigars and brandy, to come up. The reaction of the prim and pursed society ladies to de Stäel's affrontery made such an impression on young Sophia that as an adult she would delight in teasing her female guests whenever she found herself confronted by the same debilitating delicacy.

Sophia's most notorious prank took place at the base of the cliffs near Tower Bay, where she had organised a luncheon party of pigeon pie and champagne in a sea cave lit from above by a shaft. The party had proceeded in high spirits until someone noticed that the tide had turned. There was, Sophia insisted, no need to be concerned. They had plenty of time.

Among Sophia's guests that day, was Frances Power Cobbe. Frances had, by this time, effectively turned herself into her invalid mother's stay-at-home housekeeper in order to pursue her self-directed studies in history, literature, geometry, astronomy, philosophy, and writing. She had also, quite recently, abandoned all interest in orthodox Christianity, leaving her with what she called 'a *Tabula Rasa* of faith'. She described herself at the time as an agnostic and, of all those present on that day, she was perhaps the only lady with whom Sophia could share a joke, or indeed a confidence. On this occasion, however, even the redoubtable Frances was kept in the dark.

Taking their host at her word regarding the turn of the tide, the dinner party continued for another half hour, until somebody wandered towards the mouth of the cave and discovered that the tide was now 'beating at a formidable depth against both sides of the rocks which shut in the cave'. In the ensuing panic the men searched the cave for a ladder and at one stage even considered climbing the shaft to the upper cliff to get help.

As the water crept further into the cave the entire ensemble began to entertain the prospect of drowning or having to spend the night. Then, as if from nowhere, Sophia's boat appeared at the mouth of the cave. The whole incident, apparently, had been planned by Sophia who, according to Frances Power Cobbe, could not resist the temptation of infusing a little 'wholesome excitement' among her country guests.

By 1853, Sophia's health had so seriously declined that in January of that year her husband's brothers instigated legal proceedings aimed at overturning Hampden Evans' will and seizing control of the Portrane estate. The case was thrown out. Shortly afterwards, in the company of Delia Stewart, Sophia departed for France to seek expert medical care, but to no avail. She died, in Paris, on 24 April 1853, at the age of seventy-three.

Following Sophia's death, her nephew, Henry Parnell, hastened to Paris to arrange for her body to be returned to Portrane, where she was buried alongside her husband at St. Catherine's Church. Despite the body being in a lead coffin, her little terrier, according to local legend, somehow sensed her presence and fell into such a frenzy of grief that his hysteria spread to the other dogs. For fear of rabies, all six of them were shot. In her will, Sophia left a gratuity of £70 to William Kelly and stipulated that £1,000 be invested in specified stocks from which the annual interest would be used to help run the primary schools that she had founded. A small amount continues to be paid to this day.

After Sophia's demise, the lands being on an expiring lease, the estate eventually passed out of the family hands and into the ownership of the Board of Control for the Erection of Lunatic Asylums. The site was given over, in 1896, for the construction of St. Ita's Mental Hospital, with Portrane House initially serving as the home of the Medical Superintendent, before being demolished in the 1950s. The tower that Sophia built for George, however, outlasted them all and stands today neglected and forgotten.

No mention remains, either on or near the tower, of the man in whose memory it was built, of his family's role in the 1798 rebellion, or of the indefatigable woman whose profound love for her husband drove her to have it commissioned in the first place. The dedication to George Evans disappeared with the bust, which currently lies in a garden in South Wales, having been removed in the mid-twentieth century by Sir Edward Evans Pritchard, a professor of social anthropology at Oxford University. Pritchard, a descendant of the Evans family who famously converted to Roman Catholicism in 1944, did at least give the tenants of the estate a chance to view the bust before its removal. There is similarly no plaque or any other form of public information to recall the tower's status as the first of the replica memorials. The tower's sole identifier remains an untitled family crest with three boars' heads and a fading motto of 'Libertas'.

The Evans' family gravestone lies similarly forgotten, broken and weathered to illegibility within the ruins of Saint Catherine's church – small thanks for all they did for the cause of female education in the village, for their generosity during the famine, for the family's role in the 1798 rebellion, or for Hampden Evans' attempt to bring prosperity to the area by building, largely at his own expense, a quay and a salt house at Portrane, in a failed attempt to attract shipping and fishing boats to the peninsula. A small section of the salt house wall can still be seen, but little remains of the abandoned quay.

The Evans Family Grave Today.

It was perhaps a blessing that Sophia never lived to see Daniel O'Connell's tower become something of a tourist attraction while her husband's was left to decay and dereliction on a patch of wasteland, abandoned by his fellow Fingallians and diminished by the adjacent construction of an unsightly concrete water tower that adds little to the visual amenity of the headland.

Sophia Evans had met two Queens, the divorced wife of a King, and possibly even the Emperor and Empress of France; she had met the influential Madame de Staël and befriended the radical feminist Margaret King Mount Cashel; she had been a close friend of both the Darwin and Condorcet families and a daughter and sister to three of the most talented Irish politicians of her day; she had founded two primary schools in Donabate and had helped in no small way to mitigate the effects of the Great Famine in her locality. She had also been a friend and mentor to another freethinking young local woman who would go on to achieve fame within the embryonic animal rights and English suffragette movements and lead the fight for equality in education.

Sophia's achievement in reviving a tradition of tower building that had lain dormant for seven centuries lies similarly unmarked and unremembered and yet, were it not for her example, it is possible that the replica and memorial towers that now grace such diverse locations as Glasnevin, Ferrycarrig, Larne, Melbourne, Massachusetts and Flanders would never have been built, let alone the wooden replica that was famously constructed on Dublin's College Green for the duration of the Eucharistic Congress of 1932.

The tower at Portrane is hardly the Taj Mahal, but even as a posthumous love token or local landmark so treasured for years as a navigational aid by local shipping, surely it deserves a better fate than dereliction for in many respects, it stands as a greater monument to the formidable lady who built it than it ever did to her husband.

THE TOWER

Based loosely on the design of the round tower adjacent to Saint Brigid's Cathedral in Kildare Town, the Evans monument still stands today. Seated on a concrete base, it towers 100 feet above the surrounding fields with a door situated approximately 15 feet above ground surmounted by the armorial bearings of the Evans Family. Like the tower in Kildare, the lower section below the door is constructed of granite ashlar that contrasts starkly with the more traditional and less evenly coursed limestone walls above.

The tower is topped with a corbelled conical stone roof, unlike Kildare which was castellated during restoration in the 1730s. The top floor, as in the ancient towers, contains four windows orientated towards the cardinal points. On the floor below is a solitary window which, like the door, points northeast. Below that another window points to the southeast. All possess round-headed openings with granite ashlar dressing.

A SCANDAL AT LUSK

IN 1846, THE church and round tower at Lusk became the focus of a very public dispute between the Ecclesiastical Commissioners in Dublin Castle, and a newly formed pressure group that called itself the Celtic Athenaeum.

Indicative of a growing assertiveness in the expression of Irish identity amongst the middle and upper classes, this highly emotive dispute was fought out, not in the formal confines of the courts of law, but in the letters and opinion columns of newspapers and journals and, in particular, in the pages of a staunchly nationalist but non-denominational publication called the *Nation*, at that time closely associated with the rebellious Young Ireland movement.

Adding no little spice to the mix, and the somewhat patrician nature of the scandal, was the fact that the entire dispute took place against the backdrop of the Irish potato famine, when the Catholic poor had far more to be worrying about than the preservation of historical monuments.

At stake was the preservation of the round tower and medieval monastic site in the village of Lusk in north County Dublin. The monastery, which had been founded in the final years of the 5th century by Saint Mac Cuillinn, was thought by many public figures, on both sides of the religious divide, to have had a history worth preserving. The presence of a 10th century round tower on the site was particularly significant to the attention the dispute would receive, for Ireland was at the time undergoing a revival of interest in all things 'Celtic' and round towers had already assumed an emblematic and iconic status among nationalists and separatists.

The history of the monastery was a violent one. 180 people had been burned alive there by the men of Munster during a raid in 1089. A similar massacre had been inflicted by the men of Meath in 1133. Despite such raids, the monastery and round tower had survived, and the town that had grown around them had slowly grown in importance. By 1294 it had become so prosperous that the benefices of the townland were gifted by Edward I of England to the Spanish king, James I of Aragon, nephew of Edward's first wife, Eleanor of Castile.

The monastery was finally abandoned during the reign of Henry VIII, but at the start of the 16th century the medieval church was rebuilt and the round tower incorporated into the corner of a fortified Norman belfry. Three further circular turrets were built on the other three corners of the belfry to give the building solidity and symmetry. The round tower was no longer freestanding, but it nevertheless represented the sole surviving architectural remnant of the medieval monastery.

As the religious centre of a prosperous town, the monastery had *never* been insignificant and, had the site simply been an abandoned ruin, it might have been easier to secure its preservation. But the site was still in use in the early 19th century and if its eight-hundred-year-old round tower was beginning to show signs of decay, it was in nowhere near as perilous a state as the adjacent 16th century church.

Lusk Round Tower in 1791.

Matters were brought to a head by the hurricane of 6 January 1839. This storm, which destroyed up to a quarter of the houses of Fingal, blew the roof of the old church at Lusk, leaving the three-hundred-year-old building irreparably damaged. The declining Anglican congregation, which had struggled for years to maintain the building, was forced to concede defeat. By December 1845 the church's parishioners had been instructed to attend the Anglican church at Balrothery while the Ecclesiastical Commissioners in Dublin Castle set about building a replacement.

In the meantime, national interest in the origins of Ireland's round towers had exploded, ignited in no small measure by the decision of the Royal Irish Academy to hold an essay competition on their purpose and origins. In February of 1845, this competition inspired a certain Charles Byrne to undertake some amateur excavation at the tower in Lusk. In a letter addressed to the Royal Irish Academy, that was subsequently reported in the *Freeman's Journal*, he reported the discovery of the bones of jackdaws and a human skeleton embedded in yellow clay.

On behalf of the Academy, Sir William Wilde regretted the manner of the excavation and the presentation of the skull. The condition of the bones when found, he lamented, could never now be determined, nor could the means by which they had come to be there, though he suspected that the towers may have been used as a dumping ground for the remains of disturbed or collapsed graves. It was also to be regretted, he noted, that the workmen who had made the discovery had been left to work the site unsupervised.

The 'excavation' incident at Lusk resulted in an elevation of public sensitivity to the destruction of the country's archaeological heritage, and so, in November 1846, when rumours began to circulate that the Ecclesiastical Commissioners had signed contracts for the demolition of the 16th century church, and had given the builder permission to simply dump or re-use whatever he demolished, historical monuments included, the response was immediate, vehement and highly charged politically.

These rumours, reported in the pages of the *Nation* newspaper, prompted the intervention of the newly formed Celtic Athenaeum. Founded in 1845 by John O'Daly, Samuel Henry Bindon, and others from within the ranks of Irish Archaeological Society, the Celtic Athenaeum counted amongst its committee such literary giants as the poet Sir Aubrey de Vere, the novelist Walter Sweetman, and nationalist politicians of the calibre of Isaac Butt and Daniel O'Connell.

On 7 December 1846, the secretaries of the Celtic Athenaeum, Sam Bindon and Robert Webb, wrote to the Ecclesiastical Commissioners seeking to ascertain if the report in the *Nation* was founded in fact. Saddened by the proposed 'demolition of a very old and singular church, and the substitution of a small and not very beautiful building in its stead', the Athenaeum expressed particular concern about reports that one of the terms of the contract was that 'the old church is to be taken, the materials to become the property of the contractor, and the *rubbish* to be removed or levelled'.

Bindon and Webb even went so far as to suggest that that the historical monuments at risk could be saved by simply restoring the current church. This, they claimed, could be done as cheaply as building a new one from scratch. Privately, others were similarly concerned for the fate of the round tower, fearing it might be damaged during the demolition of the church, or during the subsequent building works, though this was not explicitly stated in the initial letters.

But the Commissioners had a problem. The damaged church had already proved itself too large to be sustained by a small congregation. Restoring it would have been like throwing good money after bad. Barely a month previous, at a meeting of Dublin Corporation, a certain Councillor Reynolds had joked that the Ecclesiastical Commissioners were currently 'building gorgeous Protestant churches where there are no Protestants to frequent them'. And so, to head off the Athenaeum, and prevent further interference in their plans, the Commissioners decided to act quickly, and covertly.

Lusk Round Tower today.

Having heard nothing from the Commission for a fortnight, a delegation from the Celtic Athenaeum took it upon themselves to march down to the offices of the Ecclesiastical Commission on Merrion Street and demand answers. Thomas Bushe, the Commission secretary, referred them to the Board's architect, Joseph Welland, who refused to divulge any details of the Commission's plans or to let the delegation view the contract, which they had assumed would they would be entitled to inspect as it was allegedly a public document.

Alarmed by the defensive and deflective answers they were being given, the delegation hastened to Lusk, where they found the old abbey already demolished and the cut stones of grey and red sandstone, which had formed the windows and arches of the old building, lying scattered and broken about the graveyard. Of the many ancient sepulchral monuments, only those of Sir Christopher Barnewall of Turvey, and Sir Robert Echlin of Rush, had survived the destruction, and even these had been left exposed and unprotected from weather or accidental damage, strewn amongst the rubbish of the works in progress.

The delegation noted that the belfry and round tower did not appear to have been unduly damaged during the demolition. However, as the new church occupied a different part of the site, they could also find no good reason for the demolition of that part of the building that had protected the sepulchral monuments. Much of the destruction appeared to have been wanton.

Under pressure from the increasingly virulent media campaign being waged against them, the Ecclesiastical Commissioners sent a brief and curtly worded statement to the Celtic Athenaeum, indicating that it was not their intention to demolish the round tower but to repair and preserve it, and that those monuments that had survived the demolition could 'be re-erected in the new church, at the expense of the parties interested'.

At the very least, the public campaign of the Celtic Athenaeum had managed to extract a promise to preserve the tower. The condescension of the commissioners, however, had served only to agitate them further. On 6 January 1847, an opinion piece on the dispute was published in the Dublin Evening Mail and picked up over the following days by many of the national and regional newspapers. The tone of this letter, written at a time when the Young Ireland movement was rapidly gaining in popularity, significantly raised the temperature of the dispute:

The Destruction of Lusk Church.

An act of vandalism has been perpetrated which would almost incline us to believe we were not living in the nineteenth century, or in a country in which civilisation is supposed to have made some progress, at all events among the upper classes.

The ancient abbey, long used as the parish church of Lusk – one of our most interesting ecclesiastical remains – has been, with the exception of the tower, which proved rather too tough for the despoilers, levelled to the ground, and all its fine historical monuments of the baronial and knightly families of the Barnwells, De Berminghams, and Echlins, recklessly scattered about.

To the Ecclesiastical Commissioners, we understand, this final demolition is due; but before they gave the finishing stroke, these fine old remains were left open to the wide world and pigs and cattle were allowed to enter and desecrate the sacred precincts, and the monuments and inscriptions were at the mercy of every depredator or idle passer-by.

That the present Archbishop of Dublin should have any sympathy with the historic or ancient architectural remains connected with Ireland, would be too much to expect. But to have common decencies attended to by those under his surveillance, would not have impugned his character for mere utilitarianism.

Is there an incumbent, or are there any resident gentry in this parish or district? Has the former a voice to make the wants and requirements of his parish heard; or are the latter so totally destitute of liberal feeling, and education, as to permit an act of this kind to be perpetrated, while it only needed a little exertion and care on their part to have prevented it?

Such is the increasing public feeling with regard to the preservation of ancient works of art, that, independent of local subscriptions, a very considerable and extended public sympathy might have been confidently relied on, had the least possible exertion in the right channel been attempted. On the contrary, a shameful carelessness and apathy appear to have pervaded all those who should have been foremost in the preservation of this ancient structure and its remains; and we behold the consequences.

It is, however, now too late. We can only lament what can never be restored. The fabric has got into the tasteless and remorseless hands of the Ecclesiastical Commissioners and their ARCHITECT! – (Heaven save the mark!) – and its doom has been sealed.

We all know what public Commissioners are. A certain portion of them are ornamental titled officials – Archbishops, Bishops, and Chief Justices, who never attend except to vote a friend into a Secretary or Treasurership; and there are three or four others, who attend three or four hours daily, sit on soft chairs near a snug fire, sign papers, and draw large salaries.

No one expects anything like refined feeling, or even common sentiment, from such men. But one would suppose that their architect, or advising officer on building matters, should, at least, be a person who, from his professional education and habits, would, in such a case as the present, not run counter to all the dictates of proper feeling and taste, and commit such an outrage on that spirit which is now rapidly developing itself in favour of the historic and religious remains of our native architecture.

We are glad to observe that some gentlemen, quite unconnected with the matter, as a mere local question, have taken it up; a society called the Celtic Athenaeum, recently formed for the preservation of our ancient literature and historic memorials, have remonstrated with the official Vandals. The only reply they have obtained is equally curt and characteristic. They are informed that the commissioners are going to repair the tower (unfortunate tower), and – for the monuments of the ancient neighbouring families of distinction – they have actually not sold them to the contractors – (how honest!) – adding, that anyone interested in them may be at the expense and trouble of picking up the bits and replacing them as best they can – (how obliging and considerate!)

Such is the drift of the reply – and a pleasant foretaste it presents of what the country has to expect from such a board or such officials, unless some means be taken, by drawing down public opprobrium and indignation on their acts, to make the perpetrators feel that the best instincts of our nature and our national sympathies are not to be outraged with impunity. If it be too much to expect that the heads of departments can attend to such matters, more care must be taken in the choice of their officers and advisers. The country is bearing with considerable resignation the various disfigurements that are carried on under the name of repair by this board and their architect; but wholesale spoilation and destruction it was not prepared for, and will not quietly submit to.

We understand that a memorial to the Queen is in preparation to try and stay this system; and that all the documents connected with this particular transaction will be moved for in Parliament.

The demolition at Lusk had suddenly become symbolic of a larger issue; a stick, if you will, to beat the establishment and to encourage anti-English sentiment. Over the weeks that followed, the architect who had overseen the demolition of the church was so pilloried in the nationalist press, that the Institute of Irish Architects was forced to conduct an investigation into the matter. However, not only did they exonerate Welland from blame, they even went so far as to claim that he had made every effort to preserve the old church, its monuments *and* its round tower. In pursuing the course of demolition, they asserted, he had merely been following the instructions of the parishioners.

Such was the public furore generated by the scandal, that the Institute had the resolution absolving Welland printed, not just in the *Nation*, but also the *Dublin Evening Mail* and *Saunders News Letter*. But even that wasn't enough to put a halt to the barrage of public criticism. Indeed there was sufficient blame going around by now that even the Protestant Archbishop of Dublin, Richard Whateley, found himself fingered as a culpable party for allegedly having been more concerned with his finances than the country's heritage and culture.

As the months drifted by, letters continued to be published on the subject in the pages of the *Nation*. On 12 June it carried yet another report of a meeting of the Celtic Athenaeum in which the absolution of Welland by the Irish Institute of Architects was publicly challenged. Note was also taken of the fact that a wall from the new work had been built in contact with the ancient tower 'an interference which the architects of the older church had avoided'. The Athenaeum went on to list in detail every monument that had been destroyed, damaged, disappeared, or demolished, in this 'gratuitous work of destruction and desecration'.

The word 'desecration' was slowly beginning to gain traction in the dispute and served to heap a very different kind of pressure on the Ecclesiastical Commissioners. Playing on the Victorian value that every human burial should be for eternity, the disturbance of the tombs at Lusk allowed the Celtic Athenaeum to employ the alleged 'desecration' as a tool to bring to greater public prominence the attitude of certain influential sections of Irish society towards any part of their heritage that might be considered less than British. By December letters were being received at the *Nation* fearful of similar acts of 'vandalism' being perpetrated by Protestant bishops and landlords in other parts of the country. They, too, called on the Celtic Athenaeum to intervene.

By the end of January 1847, the scandal had reached an audience beyond these shores. A letter was published in the popular London magazine, *The Builder*, describing the destruction of the church at Lusk as a 'scandalous act of vandalism' that had been perpetrated by 'persons who should have been the first to protect this venerable relic of early days'. The correspondent signed himself 'J.K.', initials that would have been instantly recognisable to readers of Dublin newspapers as belonging to the 'Peasant Poet', John Keegan.

Since 1843 Keegan's strongly nationalist poems had been appearing in the pages of the nationalist *Nation* and *The Irishman* newspapers under those same initials by which he had achieved a degree of celebrity and notoriety. In one of these poems, *Devil May Care*, he had penned an anglicised Gaelic term *shin fane* (Sinn Féin), which became the earliest known use of this expression in a political context. Significantly, Keegan was also a close friend of John O'Daly, one of the founders of the Celtic Athenaeum. His intervention was broadly symptomatic of the political turn the issue had now taken.

Letters were also written to the London-based *Gentleman's Magazine* by James Henthorn Todd, a member of the Royal Irish Academy and co-founder of the Irish Archaeological and Celtic Society, and by the respected antiquary George Petrie. Petrie did at least concede that the Ecclesiastical Commissioners had, since the demolition, publicly committed themselves to preserving the round tower, and while this represented some degree of atonement for the destruction of the church, he found that, in most other respects, their conduct had been 'not so well deserving of praise'.

It is clear from these letters that the campaign of

the Celtic Athenaeum was causing severe embarrassment to many members of Archaeological Society, not least to the aforementioned James Henthorn Todd, who at that time was serving as both treasurer of Saint Patrick's Cathedral and Patron of the Living at Lusk. Todd, a graduate of Trinity College Dublin, was an Irish Historian and biblical scholar equally noted for his advocacy of a more liberal form of Protestantism as for his love of the Irish language. It must have annoyed him no end to see the furore over the church at Lusk being used to portray the Anglican Church as a tool of the establishment, for he himself was anything but. Indeed, Todd was something of a renegade.

Todd's opposition to the new National School System had already brought him into serious conflict with Archbishop Whateley and a fictitious letter he had composed purporting to have been written by Pope Gregory XVI to the Catholic archbishops and bishops of Ireland, had landed him in extremely hot water when the true identity of the author had eventually been uncovered.

Pilloried for deceit and abused for his liberalism, Todd had withdrawn from the field of theological debate and retreated to the library at Trinity College, where he would become instrumental in the purchase of many of the manuscript treasures housed there to this day. He is perhaps best known as the man responsible for bringing the Book of Kells to prominence and is one of the primary reasons that the library enjoys a reputation today as one of the chief libraries of Europe.

Much as he might have deplored the vandalism at Lusk and harboured serious concern for the subsequent fate of the round tower, there was precious little that Todd could do. Responsibility for the funding, building, and repairing of churches and glebe houses of the Church of Ireland, had long since been granted by law to the Ecclesiastical Commission, an agency of the Dublin Castle administration.

The liberal ecumenist at Saint Patrick's, in any case, had little in common with the current Vicar of Lusk, who more or less shared the same world view as the Castle and the Commission. All he could do was wait and pray for an opportunity to apply his influence.

The dispute at Lusk had by now brought the Celtic Athenaeum into such public notoriety that, by 1847, just one year out from the Young Ireland rebellion, the *Dublin University Magazine* was describing them as a:

'....conservator of those monuments and architectural remains which the Vandalism of modern commissioners, the working members of which are Englishmen, who possess little knowledge, and less taste and interest, in those relics, that teach the antiquary, mark the historic era, or adorn the landscapes of our native land, would destroy'.

When the construction of the new parish church at Lusk eventually began, further fuel was added to the fire when builders discovered the coffin plate of Patrick Russell, a former Catholic Archbishop of Dublin. Following the Battle of the Boyne, Russell had been tracked to a hiding place in Rush and 'imprisoned in a filthy underground cell' until 1692, when death relieved him of his suffering.

It wasn't just their own history the Protestants were now seen to be destroying. At the height of a famine that was taking the lives of millions of poor Catholics, they now risked being accused of having desecrated the grave of a Catholic martyr. With political tensions on the rise, such allegations were pure poison.

The local Vicar, however, was far from bothered with the sensibilities of nationalist or Catholic antiquaries. Preoccupied with a new wife (his second) and a newborn son, the Rev. John Potterton had his hands full. On top of his domestic pressures, Potterton had a new church to build and various famine relief committees and public works to run. A few broken tombs and headstones were neither here nor there in the grand scheme of things.

Just two years previous, approximately 75% of the potato crop had been lost in Fingal, followed by an almost complete loss in 1846. Typhoid and dysentery had quickly become rampant throughout the area and those that didn't die in their homes were dying on the side of the road or in the workhouse at Balrothery. It must have been galling for the poor of the district to see the funds of a Christian church being spent on a building that few would ever sit in, rather than on food for the starving or shelter for evicted families.

But that was not how Potterton saw it. His views on poverty as a self-inflicted wound very much mirrored the prevailing views of the English upper classes of the period and he was never shy about claiming the predominantly Catholic lower classes to be inherently lazy. In a letter to the County Surveyor in February of 1847, which subsequently ended up being included in an official report to Parliament, Potterton congratulated the Surveyor on introducing a system of piece-work for famine relief payments, whereby relief to the starving workers would be dependent on the amount of work they completed each day, no matter how weak or ill they might be feeling. This system, Potterton believed, would alter the habits of the day labourers and teach them the value of time. 'I wish all Ireland could be dealt with only on the piece-work system,' he wrote, 'and I think we would soon see a different race of people.'

Potterton wrote this, despite being well aware that a deputation of unemployed labourers from Lusk had addressed a meeting of the guardians of the Balrothery workhouse just months beforehand complaining that there were more than two hundred labourers currently unemployed in the parish of Lusk and that many of them had walked to Cashel and Mullingar seeking work on the railroads, only to be forced to return 'after eating half our clothes' because there was no work to be found. Their wives and children, they had complained bitterly, were now starving, their potatoes had all been lost, and the farmers of Lusk had no work for them. So much for laziness!

THE IRISH FAMINE—SCENE AT THE GATE OF THE WORK-HOUSE.

Designed by the aforementioned Joseph Welland, Potterton's church was finally licensed for public worship on 13 October 1847. Built abutting the east wall of the Norman belfry in an early English Gothic style with crow-stepped parapets, it was considerably smaller than the 'abbey' it had replaced. Despite all promises to the contrary, the round tower was left, apart from some minor repairs, in pretty much the same state as it had stood at the time of the old church's demolition. Another six years would pass before Todd would be able to put someone in place whose concern for the archaeological heritage of the site matched his own.

During his time as a tutor in Trinity College, James Henthorn Todd had formed a close friendship with his most able pupil, a young man by the name of William Reeves. The pair had subsequently collaborated, to critical acclaim, on Reeve's edition of *Adamnán's Life of Saint Columba* and, in 1853, Todd had badgered the Anglican Primate, Lord Beresford, into providing £300 to Reeves so that he could purchase the 9th century Book of Armagh from the Brownlow family to complete a study of it. By that time Reeves had become one of the great antiquaries of the age. But he was struggling financially at his small parish in Ballymena and facing the prospect of having to abandon scholarship altogether and return to teaching. Todd was not about to let *that* happen.

Born in 1815, in Charleville, Co. Cork, William Reeves had graduated from Trinity College Dublin in 1835 with a degree in divinity. Being only nineteen years of age, and ineligible for ordination until he was twenty-one, he decided to remain in college and pursue another degree, in medicine this time, so that he might increase his usefulness as a clergyman practicing amongst the poor. In 1837 he won the Berkeley Medal and graduated with an M.B. A year later he was appointed Master of the diocesan school in Ballymena.

Shortly after his marriage to his cousin, Emma, Reeves was ordained a Church of Ireland priest, and later, while serving as a curate in Ballymena, he would become instrumental in the building of a new Church, embarrassing his parishioners to greater donations by a personal donation of £220, which everyone knew he could ill afford, for he had, by then, a wife and eight children to support. Tragically, the first funeral to be held in the newly completed church would be that of his wife, Emma, who would die from complications two weeks after the birth of their ninth child.

As the scion of a well-connected family, Reeves had enjoyed a privileged and conservative Anglo-Irish upbringing. As a student in Trinity College, on the other hand, he had also witnessed the beginnings of the Gaelic revival, heard students singing the increasingly fashionable and nationalistic *Irish Melodies* of Thomas Moore, and seen the Irish Harp becoming a favoured drawing room instrument of upper class ladies.

With an increasing number of Anglo-Irish Protestants beginning to publicly identify as Irish rather than British, a cultural shift was now underway in Ireland and the politics of identity was becoming increasingly complex. Many Irish Protestants now struggled to assert *their* version of Irishness against a competing version that had its roots well and truly planted in the Penal Laws.

With prominent clergymen becoming slowly braver in their expression of liberal and ecumenist views, it would have been difficult for any impressionable young Protestant not to feel a twinge of Christian guilt at his privilege and to seek a place at the table of this fashionably liberal revolution. In later life, Reeves would often be seen wearing the shamrock on Saint Patrick's Day, not something that was normally done by Protestants, the shamrock having by then become associated with nationalist groups such as the United

Irishmen.

This revival of interest in Ireland's Gaelic past would eventually lead Reeves, in 1844, to his discovery of the lost site of the Nendrum Monastery and the remains of an ancient round tower at Strangford Lough. Three years later still, he became a member of the Royal Irish Academy and, to critical acclaim, published his first book: *The Ecclesiastical Antiquities of Down, Connor and Dromore.*

Reeve's compulsion to immerse himself in the detail of ancient Irish manuscripts may well have been recognised early by his superiors, who appear to have feared the consequences of promoting the shamrock-wearing curate to any office that might demand too much of his attention, or indeed of his loyalty. Despite a reputation for academic brilliance, Reeves would remain a curate for almost twenty years.

In 1857, following the success of his edition of *Adamnán's Life of Saint Columba*, the Royal Irish Academy awarded Reeves the Cunningham Medal for outstanding contribution to scholarship. The occasion gave Todd a chance to discuss with his former pupil the possibility of his moving to Dublin and, with Reeve's agreement, Todd recommended him for the vicarage of Lusk, where the Rev. John Potterton had recently passed away.

For Reeves, this meant leaving the place where he had buried his wife and raised his children, but the offer was simply too tempting to refuse. At just £170 per year the appointment meant a drop in salary but, being more suited to the needs of his children, and bringing him closer to the big libraries in Dublin, it also meant that he could continue his academic investigations. He accepted both the offer and the archaeological responsibilities that came with it.

In appointing Reeves, Todd knew that he had found the right man to protect the tower at Lusk, for Reeves, despite his privileged upbringing was very much an Irishman at heart. Where others had studied the Irish language because it was deemed a necessary evangelical tool for Protestant ministers, Reeves had studied it out of genuine love for the history of the early Irish church.

In restoring the round tower Reeves would have known that he was simultaneously attempting to restore the tarnished reputation of the local Anglican Church. The tower, already purloined as a nationalist symbol, was visible throughout the village. The preservation work would be equally so. It was a win-win situation, if a trifle expensive for such a tiny congregation.

The round tower that Reeves encountered at Lusk was complete but, like so many others at the time, it was missing its conical cap. Entered by means of an unarticulated granite door case lintelled with inclined jambs, the visitor today is met with internal floors more numerous than any other tower in Ireland. These were most likely added by Reeves, who also added the cement-coated timber roof. It was most probably also Reeves who was responsible for blocking up the battlement-facing windows on the first and fifth floors and the large south-east facing window below the top floor.

The botched restoration of the top of the tower, to which Reeves added his new roof, had possibly occurred earlier, perhaps during the demolition of the old church. Only a carbon dating of the mortar will be able to tell us for certain. But however imperfect Reeves' attempt at restoration may have been, it did its job, and the tower was duly preserved for later generations.

While engaged on all of this, Reeves remained committed to the Royal Irish Academy where he continued to hold the post of secretary. On 13 January 1862, at one of these meetings, Reeves read a paper on the history, in so far as he was able to ascertain it thus far, on 'The Round Tower of Lusk'. Reported the following day in the *Dublin Evening Mail* and later that week in the *Dublin Weekly Nation*, it was to be his final contribution to the history and preservation of this tower for, shortly afterwards, concluding a residency of just five years, William Reeves left Lusk to become Keeper of the Library at Armagh and Vicar Choral of the Cathedral. In 1886, he was finally promoted to Church of Ireland Bishop of Down, Connor, and Dromore, and five years after that, he found himself elected President of the Royal Irish Academy.

In January 1887, however, while in Dublin for a meeting of the Royal Irish Academy, Reeves caught a chill and died at a room in Campbell's Private Hotel on Molesworth Street. He was seventy-seven. A memorial service was held for him in Saint Patrick's Cathedral after which his body was brought to Armagh for burial. In 1932 a memorial tablet was erected in Belfast Cathedral to commemorate his life and works, but perhaps the greater monuments to his memory are his many literary contributions to Irish history and the round tower at Lusk that both he, and the Celtic Athenaeum, had helped to preserve.

William Reeves, Samuel Bindon, and James Henthorn Todd were all Protestant gentlemen whose families had shallow roots in Irish soil. In the case of Bindon, those roots were even Cromwellian in nature. And yet, at a time when O'Connell's Catholic Association was at its most active in equating 'Irishness' with Catholicism, these men had generously fought to conserve the very history from which others were seeking to exclude them.

THE TOWER

The first records of stone-built structures on the Lusk site were noted following a raid on the site, in 1053, by Donogh, grandson of Brian Boru. As the building of a stone tower is unlikely to have preceded the building of a stone church, and the building of round towers ceased completely after the Norman invasion, the erection of the round tower at Lusk can be safely placed in the mid-10th to early 11th centuries, at a time when Viking integration into Irish society was at its highest.

The tower, which today stands at 26.56m high (originally 32m) and approximately 16m in circumference, boasts no less than ten single-lintelled windows. Apart from those that have been blocked up, there are four on the top floor that roughly correspond to the cardinal points of the compass, a fourth-floor window that faces west, a third-floor window that faces east-south-east, and a second-floor window that faces northeast.

Over the centuries the rising level of the surrounding ground has reduced the flat-headed doorway from an original height of 4.6m above ground to its current height of 90cm. Apart from William Reeves' restoration work which, despite his good intentions, is far from sensitive in sections, no further alterations were made to the tower until 1977, when metal grills were added to the remaining windows.

A similar-looking tower exists at Balrothery, attached to the corner of a rectangular Norman belfry. But the architecture of the windows and structure generally suggests a much later construction, perhaps even as late as the 16th century. The internal architecture, furthermore, shows it to be a circular turret with a spiral staircase that is integral to the belfry. It is not the remains of a round tower.

THE HUGUENOT'S CROSS

THERE CAN BE scarcely an adult alive in the twenty-first century who is unfamiliar with the term 'refugee'. The word is not a modern one, having been first coined in reference to the tens of thousands of Huguenot Calvinists who fled religious persecution in Catholic France during the 17th century. Initially seeking sanctuary in the Protestant countries of Europe, many of these *réfugiés* subsequently ended up in Ireland, where they would proceed to make a significant impact on the cultural and commercial life of the country.

The mindset and culture of these 'Huguenots' had been forged way back in 1517 when Martin Luther nailed his ninety-five theses to the door of All Saint's Church in Wittenberg to launch what would come to be known as the Protestant Reformation. Following in Luther's footsteps, John Calvin, a Frenchman, began to encourage people to break their ties to the Roman Catholic Church and embrace a new form of Christian worship focused on a personal relationship with God. Calvin's followers, drawn primarily from the French middle classes and guilds of skilled artisans came to be called 'Huguenots'. The origin of the term is disputed.

The Wars of Religion between Catholics and Huguenots that followed lasted for more than 30 years and reached an early peak in the slaughter of thousands of French Huguenots in a frenzy of Catholic mob violence on St. Bartholomew's Day, 1572. Estimates of the dead still vary wildly from a low of 5,000 to a high of 30,000.

The conflict ended in 1598, when a Protestant king, Henry IV of France, gave legal protection to the Huguenots in the Edict of Nantes. The Huguenots, however, could never truly feel secure in French society as the Edict hadn't changed Catholic attitudes and, in 1610, when Henry was assassinated and the Catholic Louis XIII took the French throne, the persecution resumed with a vengeance.

The fall of the Huguenot stronghold of La Rochelle in 1628, more or less sealed the fate of the Huguenots and led to a flood of Calvinist refugees fleeing for the safety of Protestant communities elsewhere in Europe. Over the course of the following half-century, some 10,000 of them would settle in Ireland, where their arrival was initially welcomed by a Protestant establishment only too aware of the demographic challenge facing them on a predominantly Catholic island.

The welcome, however, was somewhat cooler amongst the population at large, for whom their presence represented a threat to jobs, standards of housing, public order, morality, and hygiene. People even complained about the fact that they ate strange food and spoke a foreign language amongst themselves. In short, like all immigrants, they were new, and they were different.

In time many of these families would integrate so successfully into Irish society as to become prominent figures in the civic and commercial life of the city of Dublin. Their enrichment of their adopted city is remembered to this day in many of Dublin's street names (e.g. Mercer, D'Olier, Digges, and Fumbally) and by a plaque on a wall of the Huguenot cemetery at Merrion Row, just a few metres from the northeast corner of Dublin's St. Stephen's Green.

The Huguenot Cemetery (1695) on Merrion Row

No Dublin street bears the name of Scardeville, but that is not to say the Scardevilles did not leave their mark. Having fled initially from France to England, they had subsequently been head-hunted for their textile manufacturing experience by James Fitzthomas Butler, the first Duke of Ormonde, and made their first home in Ireland in the village of Chapelizod, some forty miles south of the city of Dublin.

Though born in Salisbury in southern England at a time when it was the centre of a thriving broadcloth manufacturing industry, Henry Scardeville received his early education 162 miles away at a free school in Repton, South Derbyshire, before leaving England in his late teens to travel to Dublin, where he enrolled in Trinity College in 1673. He came to Ireland, one suspects, primarily because of a familial relationship with a certain Joseph Scardeville, who had been hired by the Duke of Ormonde to assist him in establishing a Huguenot textile industry at Chapelizod.

During the twelve years that Ormonde had spent in exile with King Charles II of England, he had been impressed by the Parisian Huguenots' gifts for enterprise and industry, especially in the fields of textile manufacturing, watchmaking, and banking. Following the restoration of Charles II, therefore, he set out to recruit these same Huguenots with a view to establishing a modern European economy in Ireland.

Upon his return to Dublin Castle as Viceroy, and following the passing of the 1662 *Act for encouraging Protestant-strangers and others, to inhabit and plant in the kingdom of Ireland*, Ormonde invited some two hundred Huguenots from all corners of Europe to come to Chapelizod, where he established a textile manufacturing operation under the supervision and management of one Joseph Scardeville, described in the documentation of the period as a 'naturalised Frenchman'. It was most likely with Joseph, or at least at his invitation, that the teenage Henry Scardeville came to Ireland.

The atrocity stories that had circulated in Europe following the 1641 massacres of Protestants in Ulster, had stifled both migration and investment in Ireland. Lucrative incentives were therefore needed to convince families like the Scardevilles to resettle in a largely Catholic country that was only barely under the control of a Protestant government. But lucrative they were. For a twenty-shilling fee, foreign Protestants could be admitted as freemen of Dublin, and those unable to afford that could be admitted free of charge to the Guilds and Corporations, given free naturalisation, and granted an exception from paying taxes for a seven-year period.

Attracted by the promise of profit and privilege, Joseph Scardeville had been amongst the first to arrive and, in the latter half of 1662, he was granted the patents of Alnager (an officer who inspected and attested to the measure and quality of woolen cloth), and Leather Saymaster (a similar role for leather). As the patent of Saymaster is recorded in the State Papers of 1691 as a sinecure held in trust for Henry following the death of Joseph, we can safely assume a familial relationship, but it was not a paternal one. On his matriculation papers at Trinity College, Henry listed his father's name as 'James'.

An intelligent young man, whose family had invested heavily in his education, Henry Scardeville never nurtured any ambition of following in the family business. From the time of his matriculation, his sights were set on higher goals. To achieve them he needed to conform, both socially and spiritually, to the norms of Anglican society. As luck would have it, his timing was perfect.

Fearful that the Huguenots, whose religious beliefs were more closely aligned with Presbyterianism than with the Church of Ireland, might swell the ranks of Protestant dissenters against the Established Church, Ormonde had recently begun to formulate schemes to assimilate them into Anglo-Irish society such as arranging to have the Book of Common Prayer translated into French, and establishing the First French Conformed Church at the Lady Chapel of St Patrick's Cathedral in Dublin.

With the key to Huguenot advancement now lying in religious conformity, eighteen-year-old Henry Scardeville enrolled in Trinity College Dublin to study Divinity. It was a brave decision, and one that would have set him apart from his Huguenot peers. but it was soon validated when, in 1670, with Ormonde once again dismissed from his post as Viceroy, an increasingly militant Catholic population began to turn on the Huguenots, leaving them dependent for protection upon an Anglican community already suspicious of their religious allegiances.

Having graduated in the spring of 1677 and gained his Masters in the summer of 1680, Henry went in search of a parish and, in the aftermath of Ormonde's return to favour, secured an appointment as Protestant Rector of Swords and Cloghran. A year later, following his marriage to one Mary Molesworth, he was promoted to Prebendary and Vicar of Swords. At twenty-six years of age, and secure in his employment, he should have had every reason to feel happy and hopeful for the future. But there was a fly in the ointment!

The accession of William of Orange to the British throne had raised racial and religious tensions in Ireland to boiling point. His new Protestant parish, furthermore, lay a good nine miles from Dublin Castle and was surrounded by a large and increasingly militant Catholic population. The risk of a rebellion was increasing daily and, as a French Huguenot, he had ample reason to be fearful of Catholic uprisings.

But what, you might well ask, has any of this got to do with the round tower?

Well, quite a bit actually, for at a time of burgeoning Jacobite sympathies, Henry Scardeville suddenly decided to restore his new parish's round tower and, without any historical precedent, to add a small cross of his own to the cap of what, even then, was recognised as a historical monument. He did this, he claimed somewhat lamely, to remind future generations that the tower at Swords was of Christian rather than Pagan origin.

As a graduate of divinity Scardeville could scarcely have been unaware of the Columban origins of his new parish and, as the local vicar, he would have been well aware of the fact that the bodies of Brian Boru and his son, Murrough, had been waked here following the Battle of Clontarf, an act that suggests the monastery to which the tower belonged had once functioned as the ecclesiastical capital of the area.

And then there was the matter of the holy well. The worship of wells had been so common in Ireland when the first Christians arrived that they, in common with many pagan temples and druidic practices were, as the antiquary William Reeves once observed, 'made over to the aid of the new religion'. According to local legend, Saint Columcille, when founding the local monastery, had blessed the local well and given it the name of *Sord* (meaning clear or pure) from which the town had taken its name. He then gifted a holy book to Saint Finian the Leper and made him the first abbot of the monastery. As a consequence of this tradition, water from the well had for centuries been prized as a cure for leprosy and sore eyes. All of this was common knowledge locally. The Christian origins of the site would have been widely known and celebrated.

The tower itself had similarly been a constant of the local landscape since the 10th century, and one of the few buildings to have survived the subsequent centuries of conflict. Strategically important to the defense of Dublin, the town had been frequently targeted by Viking and Irish kings alike and burned on average every nine years between 1016 and 1069, and a further three times between 1102 and 1138. Despite the almost continuous conflict, the tower had survived relatively intact and, as the last surviving remnant of the old monastery, had retained a connection to a Gaelic Christian past that was unlikely to have been forgotten by the local population, let alone by their priests. It would be ludicrous to suggest that a predominantly Catholic population would need to be reminded that their round tower was Christian in origin, even if it currently stood within the grounds of an Anglican Church. So, what exactly was Scardeville playing at?

The Round Tower at Swords

Like most Protestant ministers of his day, Henry Scardeville had left Trinity College well-schooled in the exploitation of Irish history and culture as a tool of Protestant evangelism. At Trinity, his education had been shaped to a large extent by the teachings of the late Archbishop of Armagh, James Ussher, who, back in 1639, had famously claimed that the practices of the early Celtic Church represented a form of proto-Protestantism.

Ussher had used this assertion to justify his claim that Protestantism did not so much represent a split from the glorious tradition, as a return to a golden age of Irish ecclesiastical history and an uncontaminated version of Christianity. To many Protestants the round towers had since come to be emblematic of their roots in Gaelic society; a common Christian heritage that they were entitled to embrace; a justification of their presence, and privilege, in what was effectively a foreign country.

Dependent upon the whims of the Church of Ireland elite, Henry Scardeville's future was not entirely secure. Many Protestants continued to view Huguenots as closet Calvinists; an assumption that was not entirely without foundation. The French-speaking Calvinists who flooded into Ireland after 1681, furthermore, had proved to be much more militant than the first wave of Huguenot refugees in their resistance to persecution, and far less amenable to conforming to the Established Church.

In 1683, for example, the Duke of Ormonde was forced to clamp down on them for deserting the French Church at Saint Patrick's Cathedral to make common cause with the Presbyterians. As a result, their non-conformist French preacher was imprisoned and deported, and their communities were broken up. As a newly minted Church of Ireland Vicar of Huguenot extraction, Scardeville would most likely have felt a need to demonstrate his loyalty to his new congregation.

The round tower at Swords no longer functioned as a bell tower and served no practical purpose to Scardeville, other than the symbolic. In restoring the tower, he effectively claimed a degree of ownership and made a show of his loyalty to the parish. In placing his mark upon it with a cross, he attempted to root both himself and his newly acquired Anglican faith firmly within the Christian history of the village. In so doing, Henry Scardeville became the first person in the modern era to recognise the totemic nature of these towers and their proselytising potential as a symbol of continuity.

Swords Round Tower & Church by Francis Grose 1790

This was far from a simple restoration. The cross he commissioned for the roof was put there for a reason. It might just as well have been a flag. His opportunism in this matter was far from an isolated example and would be mirrored in others, most especially during the Williamite Wars and their immediate aftermath.

In 1687, just two years after James II ascended the throne of England as a Catholic monarch, the Catholic Earl of Tyrconnell was appointed as his Lord Deputy in Ireland, an act that sent some 1500 Protestants fleeing from the country in fear of retribution. Those who chose to remain were often viewed as fifth columnists. The Dean of St Patrick's Cathedral was imprisoned for transmitting information to the Williamites, while other notable Protestants were suspected to have begun corresponding with the commander-in-chief of King William's expedition to Ireland, Friedrich von Schönberg, the first Duke of Schomberg and, like Henry Scardeville, a Huguenot.

When Tyrconnell's government expelled the fellows and students of Trinity College Dublin, closed the university, and turned it into a Jacobite barracks, Henry Scardeville took stock of his situation in Swords and judged it precarious. In William of Orange he saw, not just a ray of hope, but a glimmer of opportunity. In July of 1689 then, abandoning his parishes and benefices, he fled north to join Schönberg, not as a soldier, but as his personal chaplain.

Over the course of that same year, Joseph Scardeville would find himself conscripted into the Lord Lieutenant's Company of Foot as an infantry captain. He would die the following year, as would the Duke of Schomberg, at the pivotal Battle of the Boyne. Schomberg's son, Meinhardt, would inherit his father's chaplain and both he and Henry Scardeville would survive the remaining skirmishes to enter Dublin with the victorious Huguenot regiments in 1690.

Despite his return to the capital on the victorious side, Henry Scardeville resisted the temptation to resume his parochial duties, preferring instead to remain within the protective shadow of Meinhardt von Schönberg, an act of 'loyalty' for which he was later rewarded with an appointment as Dean of Cloyne.

Such a promotion would have represented a significant leap up the social ladder for a humble vicar, and yet Henry refused to show up for his investiture.

There was a problem, you see, with Cloyne. The rectory of Clonpriest, which was worth about £70 annually and had for almost sixty years gone along with the deanery of Cloyne, had recently been usurped by Dean William Jephson. Without it, the deanery was, in the words of Bishop Palliser, 'a very inconsiderable thing'. A legal battle would be necessary to wrest it back and Henry Scardeville had no stomach for the fight. Leaving Bishop Palliser to plead for its re-annexation, Henry made an excuse of pressing 'duties' with His Majesty's forces in England and managed to avoid putting in the necessary appearance for his investiture for another five years!

There may well have been a grain of truth to Scardeville's claim to more pressing duties, though it is hard to envisage a mere chaplain being so highly valued by an army, or so dearly cherishing a military campaign. The fact that he had to petition the Treasury in 1692 for payment of the £53 he felt he was still owed from his time as chaplain to the deceased Duke, would suggest that his decision to persist with the military in preference to the church was a strategic one. Henry was looking to the future, intent on securing a place within Meinhardt's household.

Henry Scardeville's sycophantic attachment to Meinhardt von Schönberg was understandable in the circumstances and the pair appeared to enjoy a genuinel, if unequal, friendship. This may well have been rooted in their common experiences as the French-speaking sons of Huguenot refugees, but it may equally have had its roots in the general suspicion of Huguenot religious allegiances that persisted in English and Irish society.

For Meinhardt, the presence of an Anglican vicar among his household may well have gone some way to allaying suspicions of disloyalty. In return, he could, and seemingly did, open potentially lucrative doors for the chaplain he had inherited from his father. Henry Scardeville was not about to abandon all of that for the deanship of a minor Irish cathedral.

Following the Battle of the Boyne, Meinhardt von Schönberg continued in military service in Flanders, France, and Italy and, following the death of his brother, Charles, at the Battle of Marsaglia, inherited the title of Duke. The inheritance made him one of the wealthiest men in England. It also brought him within the orbit of the royal family (who would so value his company that he would be one of the six dukes invited to support the pall at William's funeral in 1702).

Milking Meinhardt's patronage for all it was worth, Henry Scardeville even went so far as to name his firstborn son, Frederick Maynhard (i.e. Friedrich, Meinhardt), in honour of his patrons rather after than his own father, as would have been customary. He would also play a small part in the naturalization process that led to Meinhardt being made a British citizen by act of parliament in April 1691.

Ireland, and indeed Cloyne, were far from Henry Scardeville's mind at this point in time. Truth be told, apart from some vague nostalgia for his first parish in Swords, where his first wife lay buried, Henry Scardeville had no great love for Ireland, or the Irish. Nor had any of his family.

In 1682 Henry had married Mary Molesworth, daughter of the infamous Colonel Guy Molesworth, a former treasurer of the Isle of Barbados. Molesworth, while serving under the first Duke of Schomberg in the war for Portuguese independence, had once narrowly escaped execution following a dispute with a certain Major-General Christopher O'Brien, brother of the Earl of Inchiquin.

O'Brien had accused Molesworth of treason and collected evidence against him from other Anglo-Irish Catholics, evidence that eventually led to Molesworth being sentenced to death. Luckily for Molesworth, he had

Meinhardt von Schönberg

influential friends in Whitehall and Lisbon and the intervention of Sir Richard Fanshaw had managed to spare his life. There was certainly no great love for Irish culture, or history, in the Molesworth family.

Indeed Scardeville's racial or religious prejudices would hardly have been softened by his choice of a second wife, for when Mary Molesworth died in childbirth, leaving Henry without children, Scardeville subsequently married one Margaret Culliford, daughter of the MP Robert Culliford, a devout Protestant and vocal supporter of the penal laws. When Margaret died, in 1698, she was buried in Isleworth, London. She left Henry with two young children, a son and a daughter, to raise alone.

There is no evidence of either Margaret or Henry having ever travelled to Ireland during her lifetime. Nor, it appears, was there any pressing need to. Several previous Deans of Cloyne had paid the post scant heed and employed curates to fulfill the needs of their parishioners, and Henry's own protracted absence had certainly proved no great impediment to his subsequent appointment, in 1693, as Archdeacon of Ross. Indeed, why would any ambitious Huguenot want to leave London during the financial revolution that was evolving at that time in the City?

Following an explosion of joint-stock companies and an ever-expanding array of investable activities, stock-market speculation was rife and a new breed of businessman, the 'stockbroker', had begun to emerge. They conducted their business affairs not in a formal stock exchange but in the coffee houses of the city of London and offered, to those with the right connections, face-to-face opportunities to make a lot of money in a very short space of time.

And so it was, in 1694, that Henry became one of only a handful of investors nominally resident in Ireland to purchase shares in the newly founded Bank of England. It is difficult, in such circumstances, to envisage him viewing the patent of Cloyne as anything more than a sinecure, or the path to further advancement as lying anywhere but within the orbit of the von Schönbergs and the wider Huguenot community in London.

But it was not to last. On 9 May 1695, Meinhardt was made a privy councillor and with his citizenship secure, and his loyalty officially recognised by a court appointment, he no longer had any need of an Anglican chaplain. Scardeville, in consequence, was left with little option but to return to Ireland. He arrived in August of that same year to finally present his patent and accept his appointment as Dean of Cloyne. But he did not come empty-handed. He was by then sufficiently well-off that he could afford to gift the cathedral an expensive 18-inch-high silver flagon, and a large silver chalice and paten.

Henry Scardeville arrived in Cloyne, as he had once arrived in Swords, to find that his new parish possessed an incomplete round tower in urgent need of repair. The conical cap of this tower had long since been replaced by an ugly parapet and battlements, and the tower itself had been further damaged by a lightning strike in 1749. Unlike his arrival in Swords, however, and despite his much-improved financial circumstances, Scardeville felt no compulsion to restore this particular landmark. There was little to be gained professionally from such a gesture and his interests now lay elsewhere.

It wasn't long before Scardeville was back in London searching for potentially lucrative investments. Using his von Schönberg contacts he joined forces, in 1697, with the influential merchant Sir James Houblon and an Irish-born judge, John Hooke to invest in a company that had recently been formed by a certain Captain John Poyntz to search for wrecks in the vicinity of Tobago, where many of the Spanish treasure ships were believed to have sunk.

Earlier, in 1681, Poyntz had been commissioned by the Duke of Courland, to re-establish a colony on the island of Tobago, to which Courland held the title. Poyntz was granted 120,000 acres in return for recruiting settlers and, in 1683, he printed and issued a recruiting pamphlet that advertised the island to potential colonists as an immensely fertile place, full of many varieties of grain and with a range of fruit that was truly amazing. Alas, the Duke of Courland's claim to the island was questioned by the Crown, who worried it would attract Dutch trade and have a negative impact on the colony at Barbados. In 1684, therefore, Poyntz's ship was temporarily banned from sailing to Barbados and the early settlers were cleared from the island.

Poyntz, still hoping to make his fortune in the Indies, continued to petition the Crown, but with little success, until 1697, when he invented a machine for raising wrecks and decided to try his hand at a new venture in partnership with a company set up by Meinhardt von Schönberg, who had been granted the rights to wrecks in the area. A single find could have made them all wealthy.

But it was not to be. Scardeville never made his fortune and Poyntz would leave no real mark on history other than the fact that a certain Daniel Defoe would allegedly use the physical description of Tobago from Poyntz's 1683 advertising pamphlet to provide the physical setting for his novel, *Robinson Crusoe*.

Upon his death, in 1703, Henry Scardeville bequeathed the sum of £100 for the support of a school for the children of the 'poor Protestants of Swords'. The bequest, however, would never be paid, and the Vestry would have to sue the executor who, in lieu of cash would substitute a lease of the tithes of the parish of Killeek, one and a half miles west of Swords. This would then be subsequently handed over to the curate, the Rev. Alexander Eustace.

It was probably with the aid of funds from this lease that, sometime about 1727, Eustace had the round tower at Swords repointed, and the upper portion rebuilt.

THE

Present Prospect

OF THE
Famous and Fertile ISLAND

OF

TOBAGO,

To the Southward of
The Island of *BARBADOES.*

WITH

A Description of the Scituation, Growth, Fertility
and Manufacture of the said Island : Setting forth
how that 100 *l.* Stock in seven Years may be improved to 5000 *l. per Annum.*

To which is added

PROPOSALS *for Encouragement of all those that
are minded to settle there.*

By Captain *JOHN POYNTZ.*

The Second Edition.

LONDON,

Printed by John Attwood for the Author, and sold
by *William Staresmore* at the *Half Moon* and *Seven Stars* in
Cornhill, and at the *Marine Coffee-house* in *Birchin Lane,* 1695.

It was probably also at this time that Scardeville's small cross was replaced by the larger undecorated Latin cross that adorns the cap today and was first reported by Henry O'Neill in 1877:

'At the end of the last century the tower was repaired, being then pointed throughout. A very old man, the sexton (John Wilson), told me that he has heard his father state that, one hundred and fifty years ago, he (the father) was present when the top was repaired, and the cross put on the apex; there had been a small cross there before'.

Further unspecific repairs were made in 1775, but by the end of the century a drawing by Lutrell Wynne showed a crumbling edifice with a poorly restored roof and upper storey. By 1779 the 'restored' cap was reported as being close to collapse. The tower was restored once again in 1832, when floors and ladders were added to the internal structure.

This revival of interest, however, appears to have been somewhat short-lived and the tower was yet again left to decay, the doorway being walled up in 1839 and a second storey window pressed into use as an auxiliary doorway. By 1877 the internal ladders were found to be unusable and by the end of the 19th century the tower was covered in ivy. Photographs from 1900, however, show the tower stripped of its ivy blanket and in a slightly better state of repair.

Today the round tower at Swords remains much as it had appeared in the 1960s, hanging in there, but only just. The top storey restoration appears as fragile as ever and, despite the best efforts of winter storms and even the occasional hurricane, it is still standing. Much of the credit for that belongs to Henry Scardeville.

To Irish Protestants and Catholics, Unionists and Nationalists, the image of the round tower has continued over the centuries to make an emotional, as well as a political statement, and people of all persuasions and politics have tried to mould that sentiment in their own image. Henry Scardeville may well have been the first person in the modern era to have recognised the propaganda potential of the Irish round tower but, as we shall discover in subsequent chapters, he would not be the last.

THE TOWER

The Swords round tower currently stands 26m in height and 5m in diameter, with a circumference of approximately 16m and walls of coarsely hammered limestone 1.2m thick. The original height would have been approximately 2m higher, but over the centuries the ground has been raised around the base and it now stands at a height of just 70cm reached by two steps of modern construction. Like all round towers of the period the door faces east. It is no longer bricked up (as was reported in 1839) but is currently fitted with a metal-grilled door.

The tower has four floors and eight windows, the top four facing the cardinal points, the windows on the second, third, fourth, and fifth floors facing east, north, south, and west respectively. A corbelled roof covers the first floor and decayed timber floors are visible on the storeys above.

The window above the doorway may have originally been used for the storage or display of relics and the topmost storey of the tower is not the original but the result of restoration. The windows on this storey are arched, whereas those on the lower floors are flatheaded. The cap, too, is obviously a restoration and has a somewhat flattened appearance. It remains, somewhat conspicuously, adorned with a cross.

IRELAND'S EYE AND THE LAST ROUND TOWERS

Claudius ptolemy, a Greco-Roman cartographer living in 2nd century Alexandria, gave the name *Adri Deserta* to the small island that sits immediately opposite the harbour at Howth. To the ancient Irish this island was known simply as *Inis Faithlenn*, the grassy island. By the early Christian era, however, it had become known as *Inis Mac Nessan*, following the founding of a monastery in the late 6th or early 7th century by Dichuill, Munissa, and Neslug, the sons of Nessan, a descendant of King Colman of Leinster.

Kilmacnessan, from a sketch by Petrie, 1828.

Today the island is more commonly known as Ireland's Eye, an anglicised corruption of two Norse words: *Eria*, the name of its female owner, and *Ey*, the

Norse for island. The island church, however, which for centuries had served as the parish church of Howth, still carries the name of Kilmacnessan (the church of the sons of Nessan). Its ruins sit, somewhat intriguingly, on a site bereft of any other monastic remains; suggesting, perhaps, that the structures that must have accompanied it had been of wooden or earthen construction.

It was at this tiny island monastery, sometime during the 9th century, that the famous *Garland of Howth* was created – a fragmentary illuminated gospel that is now in the possession of Trinity College Dublin. Originally known as the 'Kerlower' (an anglicisation of *Ceithre Leabhair*, or 'Four Books'), the 'Garland' was first mentioned in the historical record in the early 1530s when the Archbishop of Dublin, John Alen, recorded the legend of Saint Nessan and the evil spirit.

Nessan, or so the story went, while reading his gospel was suddenly confronted by an evil spirit and, in the process of expelling this evil spirit from the island the gospel was thrown and lost, seemingly forever, in the sea, only to be miraculously recovered by sailors. It had been venerated as a holy relic ever since.

Roughly contemporary with the Book of Kells, the *Garland* is only about half the size of its more famous cousin, but still too large to be considered amongst the category of 'Pocket Gospel Books' to which the Books of Mulling and Dimma have been ascribed. The 86 folios of the manuscript are inscribed with the four Gospels, with the prefaces to the Gospels of Matthew and Mark decorated with a set of intricate and idiosyncratic illuminated pages. On these pages, the large initials are mixed with interlace and beasts along with images of the evangelists and their symbols (each Evangelist is traditionally associated with a living creature: Matthew is the Man; Mark is the Lion; Luke is the Calf and John is the Eagle).

The decoration of the *Garland* is believed by some to

exhibit an early Viking influence, which is not entirely surprising, the island having been used as a base by Vikings during the 9th century. When the Irish ran the Vikings out of Howth in 902 CE, furthermore, it was to this very island, or perhaps, more accurately, to the sanctuary of its monastery, that the Viking inhabitants fled. If the book had indeed been produced on the island it would suggest both the existence and tolerance of a functioning scriptorium during the early Viking period, though the quality of the manuscript would suggest a rather impoverished one.

The Garland of Howth

By 1013 Howth was again identified in the annals as a Viking village when it was raided by Máel Sechnaill. Between then and 1042, when the Viking King, Sitric, founded Saint Mary's Church in Howth the island church continued to function as the parish church of the mainland village. It would be surprising if the monastery on the island had been neither influenced nor attended by the now predominantly Christian Hiberno-Norse population of Howth.

Sometime in the 12th century, towards the end of the Viking period and shortly before the arrival of the Normans, a small rectangular church was built on the island with a vaulted chancel and a short and narrow 'engaged' or integrated round tower. At 3.6m in diameter, the base lay somewhere between those of similarly engaged towers such as those at Saint Kevin's and Trinity Churches in Glendalough (2m and 4m respectively).

Engaged towers like these represented the first real innovation in round tower design since the building of the first round towers appeared in the 10th century. The vaulted chancel on Kilmacnessan, furthermore, supported the tower at its eastern rather than its western end, where detached towers usually stood.

Freestanding and Engaged Towers at Glendalough.

What brought about this change in tower design is as yet unknown, but perhaps it was simply a matter of expediency finally gaining the upper hand on tradition. The smaller engaged towers represented a respectful nod to the past, but were much cheaper to build. They were also, quite obviously, easier to operate. Unlike the free-standing towers, the engaged towers almost certainly had rope-pulled bells and did not require the services of an *aistreoir* to climb the internal ladders to ring them. This might also be indicative of a desire to use the tower bells as 'sacring' or 'sanctus' bells, without having to send someone outside during the consecration of the host.

Kilmacnessan today.

But why had they never evolved until now? Could it really have been simply a matter of aesthetics or was there something sacred about the original design? Whatever the functional rationale, the engaged towers represented a break with tradition that serves only to enhance the mystery of their freestanding cousins. These 12th century changes, furthermore, make the tower on Kilmacnessan one of the last, if not *the* last, of the medieval round towers to have ever been built as all traditional tower building would cease upon the arrival of European architectural influences with the Norman invasion of 1171.

The church on Ireland's Eye continued to function as the parish church of Howth until 1235, when both it and St. Mary's Church on the mainland were amalgamated to form Saint Mary's Abbey, at which time the *Garland* was removed from the island to the new abbey, where it became the source of great local devotion. The island church appears, at this point, to have been abandoned to dereliction.

During the late 19th century, the crumbling remains of the tower were demolished and the ruins extensively 'restored', apparently with a view to creating an aesthetically pleasing 'new' ruin or visual amenity that could be enjoyed from the shore and safely visited by day-trippers. During this restoration, the west door was removed, but enough of the round tower had still survived to be documented on a map of 1838.

Today just 50cm of the tower remains, sitting incongruously upon the base of an arched chancel. Today the church sits unmarked and unexplained in a field of wind-tossed bracken. Only the ruins of St. Mary's Abbey, founded by the Viking King Sitric, and the name *Howth* itself (an anglicisation of the Old Norse word *Hofud*, meaning head) remain of the town's Viking past.

MYTH AND PROPAGANDA

FROM VINCENT WALDRÉ'S painting of '*Henry the II receiving the submission of the Irish Chieftains*' to the replica towers erected in Dublin during the Eucharistic Congress of 1932, all manner of organizations have sought to make a public display of their patriotism by exploiting the instantly recognisable silhouette of the Irish round tower. To Unionist and Protestant groups it represented a pre-reformation Christian heritage that was both legitimately Irish *and* British, as much a part of the iconography of the union as the Scottish thistle or Welsh dragon. To Nationalist and Catholic groups, the towers represented the resilience and ingenuity of a Celtic race burdened by continuous invasion and the persistence of the 'one true faith' in the face of heathen or Protestant repression.

For 'heathen' of course, read Viking, for that was how they have been presented to generations of Irish schoolchildren. Indeed, so rooted has that mythology become that even today, in 21st century Ireland, round towers and Viking raids continue to share a contiguous narrative in the public imagination; a narrative that is not entirely supported by the annals, or indeed the archaeological evidence of the era.

Viking raids on Irish monasteries are an undisputed

fact. But then so too are raids by Irish clans. Of more than 300 raids on Irish monasteries between the 7th and 12th centuries, approximately half were carried out by Irish forces.

Free from Roman influence, Ireland had never developed large-scale cities and towns, and social organization was largely built around the extended family or clan. When Christian missionaries began to establish monasteries in Ireland, they did so within areas controlled by these clans and were themselves controlled by them. The monastery and its lands remained in the ownership of the founding family and functioned like mini independent kingdoms, with abbots being drawn almost exclusively from the ranks of aristocratic dynasties. Appointment and succession of abbots was governed primarily by rules of inheritance. And no, you did not misread that.

Not surprisingly, when an aristocratic family got its claws into a monastery, they were the devil's own work to dislodge and, with the abbots so closely linked to royal houses, it was inevitable that the religious communities would get drawn into the rivalries, vendettas, and alliances of their clans, and into wars with, and raids against, rival monasteries. Cork fought with Ross and Clonfert, Clonmacnoise with Birr and Durrow, Taghmon with Ferns, Kildare with Tallaght, and all of them, at least initially, with the Vikings.

The abundance of weaponry in the decoration of 9th and 10th century ecclesiastical manuscripts and high crosses bears silent witness to the violent and martial nature of the age, and of the monasteries themselves. Which brings us to those horned-helmeted savages who raped and pillaged their way across the country, sending pious Irish monks scurrying for the protection of their round towers. We can at least agree on that much, can we not?

Well, not entirely.

Let's start with that helmet. No Viking ever wore a horned helmet. That particular stereotype only really took off in 1876 when Carl Emil Doepler created horned helmets for the Valkyries in Wagner's *Der Ring des Nibelungen* opera cycle. As for the towers having been built to protect the monks from heathen savages, on no less than nineteen occasions, monastery raids were recorded as having been carried out by combined Irish and Viking armies.

Many of Dublin's monasteries actually *thrived* under Viking rule. In the middle of the ninth century, for example, Olaf the White, the first Norwegian King of Dublin, decided to build a Viking fort beside the monastery at Clondalkin; a settlement that had become well and truly established by 867 CE when its presence was noted in the *Annals of Ulster*. From this point onwards the monastery at Clondalkin appears to have been continually associated with its Viking neighbours and to have been at least partly responsible for their conversion to Christianity.

The monasteries at Finglas and Kilmacnessan similarly managed to maintain their scriptoriums during the 9th century, as did the monastery at Lusk in the 10th. All of these monasteries were situated in regions under Viking control and yet, unlike in the English Danelaw, there was no collapse of church organization and none of the important monasteries of Dublin disappeared. In fact, ALL of Dublin's original round towers appear to have been raised either in, or closely adjacent to, areas that were effectively under Viking control.

Further contradicting the popular narrative is the fact that the Irish term *genti* (pagan), which was often used to describe Vikings in the Irish chronicles, declines steadily in usage from the 940s onwards, suggesting that many of the Vikings had by this time become Christian. The suggestion is lent further weight by the fact that furnished burials cease to appear in the Irish archaeological record after the mid-tenth century. As only pagans buried their dead with grave goods, this would appear to suggest that most

Vikings had become Christian in some form or other by the time the round towers of Dublin began to be built. Indeed, it is doubtful if the marriage alliances of subsequent generations could ever have taken place after centuries of Irish Christianity if both parties to the sacrament had not been, at least nominally, Christian. This takes us a very long way from the 'heathen' narrative of popular lore.

In the Liberties of Dublin, riveted to the pebble dashed wall of a non-descript warehouse on Great Ship Street, there hung until very recently, a stone tablet marking the spot where a round tower once stood. Commissioned in the late 19th century by the Rev. William George Carroll of St. Bride's church, the plaque had originally hung on the arched entrance to the old church graveyard.

The memorial plaque on Great Ship Street.

This church, St. Michael's le Pole, and its accompanying round tower, were situated at the heart of one of the most ancient parishes of the city of Dublin, the suffix *Le Pole* or *de Palude* (of the pool or marsh) referring to the natural pool formed by the tidal action of the River Poddle from which the modern city gets its name i.e. the *Dyflinn* (black pool) of the Viking period.

Postholes and bodies excavated at the site of this church have been dated as far back as the 7th century and suggest that Saint Michael's church may have been built on the site of an even earlier monastic settlement. It is not impossible, then, that the location may have housed the elusive Monastery of Dubhlinn, the early ecclesiastical centre that was mentioned in the annals of the 7th and 8th centuries only to disappear from the written records in the 9th.

A lime kiln, a mortar pit, and a well, have also been excavated from the site. These were most likely utilised in the production of lime for the construction of both the church and its round tower. The well has been dated to between 1022 and 1164, which would date the construction of the tower to the late Viking period. This again hardly seems consistent with the construction of a defensive or protective structure.

The sheer number of Viking burials with weapons that have been discovered in Dublin would suggest that the city was home to a significantly large Norse population from the very start, making it nigh on impossible for native Dubliners *not* to have had daily contact with their Viking neighbours. The discovery of culturally Irish burials with stick pins also suggests that Christian burials continued to take place close to, or within the Viking town during this period. A number of 11-12th century Viking houses have, furthermore, recently been excavated outside of the Viking city walls at Cork Street, Church Street, and Temple Bar. These may yet place the round tower at the time of its construction squarely within a rapidly expanding suburb of Viking Dublin, rather than an outlying Gaelic enclave.

THE ROUND TOWER OF ST. MICHAEL LE POLE, DUBLIN, NOW DESTROYED.

Scandinavian bodies dating to the ninth century have also been excavated at the edge of the monastic site suggesting that, contrary to popular belief, Irish and Viking families were living and burying their dead side by side long before the church and round tower were built. Again, this is hardly the type of co-existence that would have necessitated the building of a tower as a place of refuge.

And then we have the case of Rathmichael, in south County Dublin, an early medieval ecclesiastical settlement founded sometime in the 6th century by Saint Comgall. The site contains the remains of a medieval nave-and-chancel church surrounded by a ringfort which may represent the original monastic boundary. It also contains the stump of a round tower. However, it is neither the church nor the tower fragment that has made the site famous, but rather the discovery of what have come to be known as the Rathdown Slabs: a genre of carved gravestones showing a pronounced Viking influence.

These slabs, first recorded by the antiquary, Austin Cooper, at a burial ground in Stillorgan in 1781, were subsequently found throughout the Barony of Rathdown, the majority in the vicinity of Rathmichael. The slabs, which are unique to the Rathdown area, are characterised by the carved decoration of cup marks, concentric circles, centre bands, herringbone patterns, and semi-circular loops. A few contain crosses in the form of a saltire, and one, found at Killegar, contains a Latin cross situated above the more frequently found cup-and-circle motif. Other slabs, with similar motifs, were discovered at Tully, near Cabinteely in Co. Dublin and at Taney, near Dundrum.

The decorative style of the Rathdown slabs has been attributed to Viking art and associated with the Christianisation of the Viking dynasty of MacTorcaill. Many of the motifs used to decorate them have also been found on Viking silver bracelets of the period. Indeed, the Hiberno-Scandinavian settlement of Rathmichael is known to have persisted right through to the 13th century, when the lands of Rathmichael were documented as being in the possession of an 'Ostman' by the name of MacDuel.

It is this that makes the round tower, or the attempt to build one, at Rathmichael so curious. Why would a

Hiberno-Norse community be seeking to build a Round Tower? Weren't they exclusively 'Celtic' constructions?

Viking era grave slabs at Rathmichael.

Whether the Rathmichael tower had ever been completed or not, will probably never be known but, ultimately, it is of little consequence. The significance lies in the fact that it was attempted at all within a congregation of mixed Viking and Irish identity. It would perhaps be an assumption too far to suggest that the clergy of Rathmichael were themselves of Hiberno-Norse extraction, but the existence of the tower suggests, at least in this particular case, that it is possible, given the discovery of so many 'Viking' burial slabs, that 'Viking' Christians may have formed a significant part of the congregation that attempted to build it.

The timing of the construction of the round towers is obviously at variance with the popular narrative of conflict. But if these circular medieval bell towers were not raised during the early years of Viking raids, but during a period of Viking settlement and integration into Irish society, how then did the popular narrative evolve?

The answer lies partly in the search for a uniquely Irish identity, and partly in the quest for wealth and power. Nowhere is this more dramatically illustrated than in that genre of 12th century propaganda literature in which are found such works as the *Cogad Gáedel re Gallaib* ('The war of the Irish with the Northmen') and the *Caithréim Cellacháin Chaisil* ('The military career of Cellachán of Cashel'). In these works, Irish authors seek to vilify the 'pagan' Vikings who anoint and brown their arrows with:

'... the blood of dragons and toads, and water-snakes of hell, and of scorpions and otters, and wonderful venomous snakes of all kinds, to be cast and shot at active warlike and valiant chieftains.'

At a time when the Church considered a war against pagans to be inherently just, and a war between Christian societies inherently unjust, it had become common practice for Christian societies to dehumanize their enemies and portray them as pagan to legitimize conquest and have the war accepted as 'holy'. Historic Irish victories over these allegedly heathen enemies were therefore celebrated in such works in a manner designed to foment a self-serving sense of moral superiority that could justify the bringing of prosperous Viking ports under Gaelic rule.

All this propaganda, it must again be noted, was written at a time when the Viking settlers had already become urbanised, civilised, and Christian! Indeed *prior* to the Battle of Clontarf a long history of trade and marriage alliances had seen a Viking King marry the daughter of a King of Leinster, and a King of Leinster challenge the High King of Ireland by raising a predominantly Viking army against him. That particular High King, the legendary Brian Boru, had himself climbed to power on the back of opportunistic alliances with Vikings.

And therein lay the problem. By the time the round

towers of Dublin and Fingal were being built, multiple generations of trade and inter-marriage had already blurred language and religious differences and there was little that the Vikings had ever done to the Irish that the Irish had not done to each other. If a difference did exist between the native Irish and the minority Viking settlers, it lay in the fact that control of the ports had enriched the Vikings, and what they were losing politically and militarily, they were gaining in economic power and influence.

Brian Boru did not drive the Vikings from Ireland at the Battle of Clontarf. The bald truth of the matter was that, although he and his allies had managed to inflict an historic defeat on the combined armies of north Leinster, Viking Dublin, and the Viking armies of the Orkneys, Hebrides, and the Isle of Man, in the end it proved little more than a pyrrhic victory. Brian would not survive the battle and, within their own settlements, in places like Dublin, Wexford, and Waterford, the Hiberno-Norse would continue to govern as they had for centuries and to form alliances with Irish clans, upon whom they would slowly become dependent. In time, the Norman invasion would blur the lines between Irish and Hiberno-Norse and the Vikings would be so completely absorbed into Irish society that surnames like Halpin, Higgins, and Sweetman would seem as indistinguishably Irish to the native population as O'Neill and O'Donnell.

From the time of the Penal Laws onwards, however, when Irish Catholics became second-class citizens in their own country, comparisons between the acts of one group of foreign invaders with those of another became inevitable and the victory of Brian Boru at Clontarf began to appear with increasing regularity in Irish prose. With each re-telling, the 'heathen' Vikings became more unsparingly savage, while Brian became more devout, heroic, and 'Christ-like' (a tradition that he had been murdered while at prayer on Good Friday began to appear in the 16th century).

The more the Vikings were vilified, of course, the more important the symbolism of the round tower as a place of sanctuary and martyrdom became, in effect becoming almost as holy in the public imagination as the relics and monks they were once supposed to protect. There was little room in such a simplistic narrative for the two races not only sharing a common space during the era of tower building, but a common vision of eternity. There was even less room for round towers and monasteries that may actually have been built with Viking support.

Following the granting of Catholic emancipation in the middle of the 19th century, the religious iconography of the Celtic church became irretrievably entangled in the identity politics of a rapidly changing nation. Where Speed & Camden had attempted to create a unified 'British' history with maps, unionists and nationalists alike now sought to establish their 'Irishness' with symbols of an idealised and distant Christian past.

While those of a unionist disposition chose to see in such symbols a means of shaping a shared hope for the future; nationalists in their turn began to interpret them as the manifestation of a uniquely Irish 'difference'; a difference that justified a push for independence, and perhaps also, in retrospect, a providential purpose to the centuries of suffering and oppression.

For *Nationalist*, of course, you could by now read *Catholic*, for ever since Daniel O'Connell's mass political movement began to focus solely on the interests of Irish Catholics, Irish nationalism had more or less become synonymous with Catholicism. In such a climate the round tower was quickly adopted as one of the four archetypal icons of the nationalist movement, the others being the High Cross, the Irish Harp, and the Shamrock.

In 1843, when O'Connell, planned a mass meeting at Clontarf, it was with the deliberate intention of invoking the memory of Brian Boru and his victory over the Vikings. And why not? Hadn't James I allegedly once considered changing his name to Arthur? Hadn't the restoration of a supposed ancient unity always been the go-to strategy of politicians at times of social and political upheaval? Hadn't nostalgia for past glories always been the go-to source of comfort and confidence in uncertain times?

By now, of course, one could scarcely invoke the image of the Vikings without similarly calling to mind the image of the round towers, and so, in September of the following year, when six grey horses drove O'Connell in triumphant procession through the throng of 220,000 supporters that had spilled onto the streets of Dublin to celebrate his release from prison, a round tower was prominent in the decoration of the side panels of his 'chariot'.

As far back as 1787, furthermore, the Marquis of

Buckingham had commissioned the Italian painter Vincent Waldré to re-decorate Dublin Castle with three large paintings: *George III supported by Liberty and Justice, Saint Patrick converting the Irish to Christianity*, and *Henry II receiving the submission of the Irish Chieftains.*

In the latter, and most politically charged of the three, a round tower is placed prominently in the background, as indeed it was, less than a century later, in Daniel Maclise's *The Marriage of Strongbow and Eva.* Completed in 1854, the latter was commissioned by the House of Lords as part of a celebration of the acquisition of colonies by the British Empire. It was supposed to depict the beginnings of British rule in Ireland. It was also supposed to be triumphalist in nature. Within this painting, however, Maclise chose to depict Strongbow placing his foot upon a fallen Celtic cross as Diarmuid MacMurrough looks on in alarm and an elderly harpist slumps despairingly on his instrument. Triumphalism or regret? Loyalist or subliminally subversive?

In a similarly unionist vein, when the British Army sought to recruit Irish soldiers to fight in the First World War, the round tower assumed a prominent place on the recruiting posters. The posters illustrate just how politically ambiguous a symbol the round tower had now become, representing for some the history of a stubbornly 'Celtic' race that was anything but British, and for others a common Christian thread that unified the kingdoms of Great Britain and Ireland and claimed the Irish as a people no more Celtic, nor any less British, than the Scots.

By the end of the Great War, however, that ambiguity was being slowly lost as the image was appropriated by the nationalist cause. Following the founding, in 1884, of the Gaelic Athletic Association, they even began to appear in the names of newly founded GAA clubs in Clondalkin, Lusk, Kildare, and London.

British Army recruiting poster from 1915.

By now, however, a certain cynicism was beginning to creep into sections of Dublin society regarding the use of such images and the type of narrow-minded and xenophobic nationalism they seemed to encourage, not just amongst the Irish at home, but also amongst the many emigrants aboard. In 1922, the year that Ireland finally gained its independence, Joyce himself, in the Cyclops chapter of Ulysses, took pointed aim at them:

'The figure seated on a large boulder at the foot of a round tower was that of a broadshouldered deepchested stronglimbed frankeyed redhaired freely freckled shaggybearded widemouthed largenos jued longheaded deep-voiced barekneed brawnyhanded hairylegged ruddyfaced, sinewyarmed hero.'

Joyce's cynicism appeared, if not prophetic, then at least justified when, in 1933, the Irish government sent an archaeological cultural package to be exhibited at the World's Fair in Chicago. The National Museum, The Royal Irish Academy, and the Royal Society of Antiquaries of Ireland had collaborated to create an exhibit that would highlight *A Century of Progress in Irish Archaeology* and showcase the artistic and intellectual achievements of the newly independent nation. They had no sooner returned home, however, when the impression of a progressive and educated nation was all but obliterated by a subsequent exhibition.

As Irish Americans rushed to join the celebration of a country that many of them had never actually seen, they began to appropriate images of 'Celtic' Ireland in a very American way. A commercial 'Irish Village' was constructed next to the 'Midget Village' at the Chicago World's Fair with the backing of Irish-American investors, the stated aim of which was to present to the American public a representation typical of 'the life and natural activity of all the *fourteen* counties of

Ireland'. Replete with a peep show next to the shrine of Saint Brenda and girls in silk tights peddling shamrocks, it was constructed for the occasion with thatched cottages, a 'Tara's Hall', a 'Colleen Bawn rock' and a 'Stone of Destiny' (confusing Scotland for an Irish province). It even boasted a round tower, leaning of course. Wasn't that what those old European towers did?

The following month, in Soldier's Field, a lavishly produced pageant was staged to extol 'the glories of the ancient Celtic civilisation'. The poster for this event, *The Pageant of the Celt*, featured a Viking longboat with a sail emblazoned with a Celtic cross and a round tower surrounded by skyscrapers!

It had all been done so much better at the Chicago World's Fair of 1893 when two Irish Villages were established by Mrs Ernest Hart, founder of the Donegal Industrial Fund. Hart's village also had a replica round tower, with models of a cromlech, ogham stones, and early Christian crosses at its base, although, that said, over in the Agricultural Building John Power & Son, inspired by O'Connell's tower in Glasnevin, had constructed a replica round tower out of whiskey bottles!

A lot had changed in forty years and with the loss of first-hand knowledge of the country, the temptation to resort to stereotypes in pandering to a non-Irish market proved too great. The result, not a million miles from the hard-drinking, dudeen smoking, in-bred simian so beloved of 19th century British cartoonists, was no less damaging to those who sought to portray a modern, industrial, and educated country to the world.

Despite the horror of the educated classes at the type of gombeen stage-*oirishness* they saw reflected in such images, in the cosmopolitan city of Dublin round towers, both real and imagined, continued to be exploited as political and religious icons. The new country, desperate for stability, unity, and uniformity, had to be loyal to something.

The Power's Whiskey Bottle Round Tower.
Image courtesy of Irish Distillers Pernod Ricard.

But if not a king, then what? What could unite a country where the memories of a bloodily divisive civil war still suppurated in the minds of the survivors? Well, in 1932, just one year prior to the Chicago debacle, the country had given its answer. When the Catholic Church opted to hold their 31st International Eucharistic Congress in Dublin, millions had poured onto the streets in acts of such unity and pious devotion that neither politician nor cleric could ignore the implications.

The Round Tower on College Green (1932)
Photo courtesy of Independent Newspapers/NLI

With the eyes of the Catholic world focused on the city, it was decided to erect replica round towers at strategic locations such as College Green and St. Stephen's Green, for the round tower had by now become the perfect vehicle with which to equate Irish Nationalism and Roman Catholicism and to legitimize in the public imagination the historic position of the Catholic Church as the moral leader of Irish society. Catholic and Celtic, Harps and Round Towers, that was to be our story, the united face we presented to the world at large. And it would remain thus for decades.

Ireland has changed so much since the advent of the twenty-first century, that round towers no longer feature prominently in our nationalist iconography. The influence of the Catholic Church is no longer quite so significant or pervasive as it once was and new generations of migrants have arrived on our shores to face many of the same challenges and allegations that once greeted previous waves of Celts, Picts, Vikings, Phoenicians, Normans, Huguenots, Palatines, Jews and English.

Whatever their architectural origins, the round towers of Fingal or *Fine Gall* (literally 'foreign tribe') do not just represent an amazing feat of ancient engineering and design, but challenge by their very location and chronology, the popularly accepted narrative of marauders and martyrs that led to their iconic status in the first place. The ancient towers, and their modern replicas, stand both as monuments to the country's Christian past, and as a reminder of the ever-changing and complex nature of our national identity.

The fact that at least one of Fingal towers may have been built by the descendants of uninvited immigrants or invaders, and that the others have largely been preserved or built by the scions of families with notoriously shallow roots in Irish soil, serves only to remind us that, not only is difference diluted by time, but that our sense of national identity is constantly evolving and more than capable of encompassing everybody, given time. At the end of the day, we Fingallians, like so many other coastal communities, have *always* been a diverse lot. The towers also remind us of that.

Bibliography

Illustrations

Index

BIBLIOGRAPHY

THE ENDURING MYSTERY

Bolton, J. 'Irish Medieval Mortars: Implications for the formulation of new replacement mortars,' as part of *2nd Historic Mortars Conference & RILEM TC 203-RHM Repair Mortars for Historic Buildings* Prague, 22-24 Sept 2010. Institute of Theoretical and Applied Mechanics of the Czech Republic & RILEM.

Bourke, C. (1980) 'Early Irish Hand-Bells', The Journal of the Royal Society of Antiquaries of Ireland, Vol. 110, 52-66.

Bourke, C. (2013) 'Early Breton Hand-bells Revisited'. *Melanges Bernard Merdrignac*, pp.275-281.

Carew, Mairéad. 'The Quest for the Irish Celt: The Harvard Archaeological Mission to Ireland, 1932–1936'. Irish Academic Press, Newbridge, Co. Kildare, 2018.

Gottheil, Richard J.H. 'The Origin and History of the Minaret', Journal of the American Oriental Society Vol. 30, No. 2 (Mar., 1910), pp. 132-154

Lalor, Brian. 'Ireland's Round Towers – Origins and Architecture Explored,' Collins Press, Cork, 1999.

O'Keeffe, T. *Ireland's Round Towers*. Tempus. Gloucestershire, 2004.

Stalley, Roger. 'Belfries - Irish Architecture in the Early Middle Ages: c. 500–1200 AD', Media center for art history, archaeology and historic preservation, Columbia University (27-04-2018).
http://www.learn.columbia.edu/ma/htm/sr/ma_sr_discuss_ia_belfries.htm

Stalley, Roger. 'Irish Round Towers', Country House, Dublin, 2000.

Thurston, Herbert. 'Bells', in The Catholic Encyclopedia, New York: Robert Appleton Company (1907).

SOPHIA EVANS AND THE WIDOW'S TOWER

Advertiser Notes and Queries, Volume 2, 'Advertiser' Office, Cheshire, England, 1884.

Burtchell, George Dames & Sadlier, Thomas Ulick. 'Alumni Dublinenses: a register of the students, graduates, professors and provosts of Trinity College in the University of Dublin (1593-1860)', Alex. Thom & Co. Ltd., Dublin, 1935.

Chief Secretary's Office, Registered Papers, CSO/RP/1829/1409, 'Letter from C Condorcet O'Connor, [Dublin], relating to naturalisation of Arthur O'Connor's son.'

Cobbe, Frances Power. 'Life of Frances Power Cobbe', Houghton, Boston 1894.

Conner, Clifford D. 'Arthur O'Connor – The Most Important Irish Revolutionary You May Never Have Heard Of', iUniverse Inc., New York, 2009.

Darwin, Charles; Burkhardt, Frederick & Smith, Sydney. *The Correspondence of Charles Darwin: 1821-1836*, Cambridge University Press, 1985.

'Deaths', The Freemans Journal, Sat. Dec 19th, 1846; p4.

'Death of the Right Hon. George Evans', Kerry Evening Post 1813-1917, Saturday, July 09, 1842; p1., and Freemans Journal, July 04, 1842; p2.

Dictionary of Irish Architects. 'Miller, George', retrieved 23/12/2018. https://www.dia.ie/architects/view/3469/MILLER-GEORGE.

Donovan, Julie. 'Sydney Owenson, Lady Morgan and the Politics of Style,' Academica Press, LLC, 2009.

Ervine, St John. 'Parnell: His Family', Ernest Benn Ltd., London 1925.

'Evans v. Evans', in English Reports in Law and Equity: Containing Reports of Cases in the House of Lords, Privy Council, Courts of Equity and Common Law; and in the Admiralty and Ecclesiastical Courts, Including Also

Cases in Bankruptcy and Crown Cases Reserved, [1850-1857], Volume 19, Edmund Hatch Bennett, Chauncey Smith, Charles C. Little and James Brown, 1854.

Fagan, Patrick. 'Infiltration of Dublin Freemason Lodges by United Irishmen and Other Republican Groups.' *Eighteenth-Century Ireland / Iris an Dá Chultúr*, vol. 13, 1998, pp. 65–85. *JSTOR*, JSTOR, www.jstor.org/stable/30064326.

Feldman, Paula R. and Cooney, Brian C. 'The Collected Poetry of Mary Tighe', JHU Press, 2016.

Freemans Journal, 'Paris, aged 73 years, Sophia, widow of the Right Hon. George Evans, M.P., of Portrane, county Dublin', page 4, Thursday, May 5th, 1853.

'From the Farmer's Gazette', Irish Examiner Mon. Sept. 20th 1847, p1.

Geoghegan, Patrick M. 'Liberator – The Life and Death of Daniel O'Connell 1830-1847', Gill & McMillan, 2010.

Griffith, Richard. 'An address delivered at the ninth annual meeting of the Geological Society of Dublin, on the 12th of February 1840', Hodges and Smith, Dublin, 1840.

Hughes, Marie. 'The Parnell Family; Dublin Associations.' *Dublin Historical Record*, vol. 16, no. 3, 1961, pp. 86–95. *JSTOR*, JSTOR, www.jstor.org/stable/30102706.

Johnson, James. 'A Tour in Ireland; With Meditations and Reflections'. S. Highly, 32 Fleet Street, Dublin 1844.

Judge, J. 'Plain and Useful Hints for Farmers being chiefly composed of Extracts taken from some of the most Practical Publications of the Times for the Proper Cultivation of Turnips and other green Crops &c.'. Printed by George Nash, Cork, April 1847.

Keenan, Desmond. 'The Grail of Catholic Emancipation 1793 to 1829', Xlibris Corporation, 12 Nov 2002

Kelly, William. 'The crops proper to be grown at this emergency, and their culture', Leinster Express, Dec 12th 1846; p.4.

Kelly, William, 'The Irish Small Farmer of 1847; Containing Ample Directions for the Cultivation of the Soil During the Present Crisis', Cumming & Ferguson, 1847.

Lewis, Samuel. 'A Topographical Dictionary of Ireland', S. Lewis & Co., London, 1837.

Mavor, Elizabeth (ed.), 'The Grand Tours of Katherine Wilmot: France 1801-3 & Russia 1805-7, Weidenfeld, 1992.

Morgan, Lady 1783-1859. Lady Morgan's Memoirs: Autobiography, Diaries and Correspondence. Copyright ed. Leipzig: B. Tauchnitz, 1863.

Moylan, Thomas King. 'The Peninsula of Portrane: Part I.' *Dublin Historical Record*, vol. 16, no. 1, 1960, pp. 22–33. *JSTOR*, JSTOR, www.jstor.org/stable/30102698.

National Archives documents, CSO/RP/1832/4736, CSO/RP/1830/1321, CSO/RP/1830/1320, and CSO/RP/1829/1409.

'New Catholic Association', *Dublin Evening Post*, Dec. 11th, 1827, p.4.

O'Connell, Maurice R. Ed. 'The Correspondence of Daniel O'Connell, Volume IV, 1829-1832' Dublin Stationery Office for the Irish Manuscripts Commission, 1977.

Portrane Primary Schools, National Archives, ED/1/29/12-13.

'Royal Dublin Society', Freemans Journal, 19-12-1846, p12.

Sullivan, Thomas. 'On the Cultivation of Wheat'. British Farmer's Magazine, Issue 11, James Ridgway, 1847.

The Parnell Family. Otago Witness, Issue 1793, 3 April 1886.

The Court Magazine & Monthly Critic and Lady's Magazine: Volume 5, Dobbs & Co., London, 1834.

The Court Magazine & Monthly Critic and Lady's Magazine: & Museum of the Belles Lettres, Music, Fine Arts, Drama, Fashions. & c. united ser, Volume 8, Dobbs & Co., London, 1836.

The Court magazine and Monthly Critic, Volume 12, Dobbs & Co., London, 1838

Tighe, Mary. 'The Collected Poems and Journals of Mary Tighe', University Press of Kentucky, 2015

Tithe Commutation Bill. Dublin Evening Post Jan 31ˢᵗ 1824, p4.

Todd, Janet. 'Mary Wollstonecraft: A Revolutionary Life'. Weidenfeld & Nicolson, London, 2000.

Virtue, George. 'The Royal Court Guide, and Fashionable Directory, 1842, with a list of subscribers to Finden's Ports, Harbours, and Watering-Places', London 1842.

A SCANDAL AT LUSK

'An Historical Account of the Cunningham Fund'. Proceedings of the Royal Irish Academy (1836-1869). Vol. 7 (1857 - 1861).

'Answers to Correspondents'. *Nation* newspaper, 05.12.1846, p10.

Burke, Helen. *'The People and the Poor Law in 19th Century Ireland'*. Women's Education Bureau, Dublin, 1987.

'Celtic Athenaeum', the Nation newspaper, 09.01.1847, p.16.

Collins, Sinéad. 'Balrothery Poor Law Union, County Dublin, 1839-1851,' Four Courts Press, Dublin, 2005.

'Destruction of Lusk Church, County Dublin', in 'The Builder: An Illustrated Weekly Magazine', No. 204, London, Jan 2ⁿᵈ 1847.

Fogarty, Chris. *'The Mass Graves of Ireland: 1845-1850,'* Oct. 26 and Nov. 2, 1996, *The Irish People*, NYC.

Holm, Poul. 'The Slave Trade of Dublin, Ninth to Twelfth Centuries,' in Peritia, 5, Cork and Galway, January 1986, p 317.

'Lusk Church – Who is the Vandal?', the 'Nation' newspaper, 16.01.1847, p9.

Macdonald, Philip. 'Monitoring at Nendrum, Mahee Island, Co. Down,' 2003, at qub.ac.uk, web site of Queen's University, Belfast.

Moore, Norman. *'Reeves, William (1815–1892)'.* In Lee, Sidney. Dictionary of National Biog., London: Smith, Elder & Co. (1896).

O'Connell, Aidan, 'Excavations at church road and the early monastic foundation at Lusk, Co. Dublin' in C. Baker (ed.) Axes, Warriors and Windmills. Recent archaeological discoveries in Fingal. 51-63. Fingal County Council (2009).

O' Connor. J. (1995), *The Workhouses of Ireland: The Fate of Ireland's Poor,* Anvil Books, Dublin.

O'Riordan, Colum. Biographical Dictionary of Irish Architects 1720-1940, Irish Architectural Archive.

Oulton, John Ernest Leonard. 'William Reeves - Bishop, Scholar, Antiquary', Memorial Discourse, T.C.D., 24 May 1937.

Parliamentary Papers, Volume 52, Accounts and Papers: Thirty-Seven Volumes (19), Relief of Distress (Ireland): Board of Works, Part II, Commissariat, Part II, Session 19 January – 23 July 1847, Vol. LII, pp 188-189. Great Britain, Parliament, H.M. Stationery Office, 1847.

Reeves, William Rev. 'The Antiquities of Swords: A Lecture on the Antiquities of Swords', delivered in the Borough Schoolhouse Swords, 12th September 1860, St Columba (Church: Swords, Ireland), University of St Andrews. Library. Copyright Deposit Collection.

Ricorso Website. (Rev.) William Reeves biography. http://www.ricorso.net/rx/az-data/index.htm

'Royal Irish Academy', *Freeman's Journal,* 26th Feb. 1845, p3.

Simms, G.O. 'James Henthorn Todd' in Hermathena, No. 109 , Trinity College Dublin, Autumn 1969. http://www.jstor.org/stable/23039923

'The Corporation', The Freemans Journal, 9th December 1846. *'The Destruction of Lusk Church, County Dublin'*, Kerry Evening Post, 09.01.1847, p1.

'The Dublin University Magazine – A Literary and Political Journal'. No. CLXIX, Vol. XXIX, Jan-Jun, pp 357-358, James McGlashan, Dublin, 1847.

'The Ecclesiologist,' New Series, Volume IV, p.160, Ecclesiological Late Cambridge Camden Society, Joseph Masters, London, 1845.

The Gentleman's Magazine, Volume 27, W. Pickering, 1847. P.411.

'The Late Bishop Reeves', Belfast News-Letter, Nov. 1st 1892, p7.

'To the editor of the Nation', *Nation* newspaper, 11.12.1847, p10.

'Want of employment in Fingal', Freeman's Journal, 7th Oct. 1846.

Welland, Joseph. 'Dictionary of Irish Architects 1720-1940', Irish Architectural Archive, http:www.dia.ie, 25-April-2018.

THE HUGUENOT'S CROSS

'Annals of the Four Masters,' Author Unknown, Corpus of Electronic Texts Edition (UCC), https://celt.ucc.ie//published/T100005B/index.html.

Appleby, David J. 'God forbid it should come to that': the feud between Colonel Molesworth and Major-General O'Brien in Portugal, 1663, The Seventeenth Century, 26:2, 346-367, DOI: 10.1080/0268117X.2011.10555674, 2011.

Barrow, George Lennox. 'The Round Towers of Ireland'. The Academy Press, Dublin, 1979.

Bateson, Edward & Hardy, William John. 'Calendar of State Papers, Domestic Series, of the reign of William and Mary, 1 November 1691 – end of 1692. Dec 31 Kensington', Public Record Office, Kraus 1969.

Bowen, Elizabeth. 'Bowen's Court & Seven Winters'. Random House, 2015

Brady, William Maziere. 'Clerical and Parochial Records of Cork, Cloyne and Ross', Longman, Roberts and Green, London 1863.

Brash, R.R. 'Reply to Letter of Rev. Mr. Graves'. Journal of the Kilkenny and South East of Ireland Archaeological Society (Volume VI), 1867.

Burtchell, George Dames & Sadlier, Thomas Ulick. 'Alumni Dublinenses: a register of the students, graduates, professors and provosts of Trinity College in the University of Dublin (1593-1860)', Alex. Thom & Co. Ltd., Dublin, 1935.

Calendar of Treasury Books, Volume 9, 1689-1692, February 1692 21-29, p 206. H.M. Stationery Office, London, 1931.

Costello, Vivien. 'Researching Huguenot Settlers in Ireland', The BYU Family Historian, Vol. 6, Fall 2007.
Downham, Clare. 'The Battle of Clontarf in Irish history and legend', in *History Ireland*, Issue 5, Volume 13, September/October 2005, Dublin.

Downham, Clare. 'Fine Gall', in Medieval Ireland an Encyclopaedia, ed. Seán Duffy, Routledge, New York and London, 2005.

Gibbons, Patrick, 'Emerging Ireland: Antiquarian Writing and the Molding of Irish Catholic Identity in the 18th Century' (2015). *Honors Theses*. Paper 90.
http://digitalcommons.csbsju.edu/honors_theses/90

Hylton, Raymond. 'Dublin's Huguenot Refuge: 1662-1817', *Dublin Historical Record*, Vol. 40, No.1 (Dec. 1986), pp.15-25.

Lawlor, Hugh Jackson. 'Diary of William King, D.D., Archbishop of Dublin, during his imprisonment in Dublin Castle', *The Journal of the Royal Society of Antiquaries of Ireland*, Fifth Series, Vol. 33, No. 2, [Fifth Series, Vol. 13] (Jun. 30, 1903), pp. 119-152.

Lewis, Samuel. 'A Topographical Dictionary of Ireland', Lewis & Co. London, 1837.

Manning, Conleth. 'Burials', in Séan Duffy (ed.), *Medieval Ireland: an encyclopedia* (New York, 2005).

Ní Mhaonaigh, Máire. 'Friend and foe: Vikings in ninth- and tenth-century Irish literature' in Howard B Clarke, Máire Ní Mhaonaigh and Raghnall Ó Floinn (eds.), *Ireland and Scandinavia in the early Viking Age* (Dublin, 1998) p381.

Ó Danachair, C. 'In Fond Remembrance: Headstone inscriptions from St. Columba's Graveyard', No. 2; Fingal Heritage Group. 1958.

O'Neill, Henry. *The Round Towers of Ireland*, M. H. Gill and Son, Sackville Street, Dublin 1877.

Petrie, George. 'The Round Tower of Swords', from *The Dublin Penny Journal*, Vol. 1, No. 23, December 1st 1832.
Ramsay, G.D. 'The Wiltshire Woolen Industry in the Sixteenth and Seventeenth Centuries', Second Edition, Frank Cass & Co. Ltd., 1965.

Reeves, William Rev. 'The Antiquities of Swords: A Lecture on the Antiquities of Swords', delivered at Borough Schoolhouse Swords, 12th September 1860, St Columba (Church: Swords, Ireland), University of St Andrews. Library. Copyright Deposit Collection.

'Report from the Commissioners of the Board of Education in Ireland,' Act 46, GEO. III., 1809-1812, House of Commons, Great Britain, 1813.

The Registers of Cloghran Parish Church, Baptisms 1782-1864, Marriages 1739, 1782 – 1839, Burials 1732-1864. Transcribed and Indexed, Diocese of Dublin, County of Dublin, The Anglican Record Project, February 1997.

Walsh, Patrick. 'The South Sea Bubble and Ireland: Money, Banking and Investment, 1690-1721', Boydell & Brewer Ltd, 2014.

Walsh, Robert. Fingal and Its Churches: A Historical Sketch of the Foundation and Struggles of the Church of Ireland in That Part of the County Dublin Which Lies to the North of the River Tolka. W. McGee, Dublin, 1888.

Wright, G. N. & Bartlett, W. H. 'Ireland Illustrated'. London: H. Fisher, Son, and Jackson, 1831.

IRELAND'S EYE AND THE LAST ROUND TOWERS

Cochrane, Robert. 'Notes on the Ecclesiastical Antiquities in the Parish of Howth, Co. Dublin', *JRSAI*, 23 (1893), pp 386-407 at 396-403.

Downham, Clare. 'Viking Kings of Britain and Ireland: The Dynasty of Ívarr to A.D. 1014', Dunedin Academic Press, 2010.

Hiney, Diarmuid D. 'Ireland's Eye', *Dublin Historical Record* , Vol. 45, No. 2, Old Dublin Society, 1992.

Lalor, Brian. 'Ireland's Round Towers – Origins and Architecture Explored,' Collins Press, Cork, 1999.

Maps of the Society for the Diffusion of Useful Knowledge. Vol. 1, by the Society for the Diffusion of Useful Knowledge (Great Britain) (London: Chapman and Hall, 1838).

Macalister, R.A.S. 'Ancient Ireland: A Study in the Lessons of Archaeology and History', Routledge, 2014.

Vallancey, Charles. 'Collectanea de Rebus Hibernicus', Vol. 3, Luke White, 1786.

MYTH AND PROPAGANDA

Aitken, George A. 'The Life of Richard Steele', London, 1889.

Bell, Thomas. 'An Essay on the Origin and Progress of Gothic Architecture, with reference to the ancient history and present state of the remains of such architecture in Ireland', W.F. Wakeman, 1829.

Boyd, Rebecca. 'Where are the longhouses? Reviewing Ireland's Viking-Age Buildings', in Clarke, H.B. & Johnson, R. (eds.) Before and After the Battle of Clontarf: The Vikings in Ireland and Beyond: 325-45, Four Courts Press, Dublin 2015.

Breathanach, Edel, 'Communities and their Landscapes', in The Cambridge History of Ireland: Volume 1, 600–1550, edited by Brendan Smith, Cambridge University Press, March 2018.

Carew, Mairead. 'The Pageant of the Celt — Irish Archaeology at the Chicago World's Fair, 1933-4,' in Archaeology Ireland, Vol. 28, No. 1 (Spring 2014).

Corlett, Chirstiaan. 'The Rathdown slabs – Vikings and Christianity', in Archaeology Ireland 17(4; 2003), 28-30.

Crosthwaite, John C. 'The Book of Obits and Martyrology of the Cathedral Church of the Holy Trinity, Commonly Called Christ Church. Dublin. Ed. from the Original Manuscript, with an Introduction by James Henthorn Todd', Irish Archaeological Society, Dublin, 1844.

D'Alton, John. 'The History of the County of Dublin', Hodges and Smith, Dublin 1838.

'Did You Know...? Forgotten Aspects of our Local Heritage', Dun Laoghaire Rathdown County Council, Dublin, 2009.

Dodd, Charles.' The Peerage, Baronetage, and Knightage, of Great Britain and Ireland, including all the Titled Classes'. Whittaker & Co. 1846.

Downham, Clare. 'The Viking slave trade: entrepreneurs or heathen slavers?' History Ireland, Vol. 17, Issue 3, May/June 2009.

'Dublin's Round Tower', The Irish Times, March 20th 1930.

Fallon, Donal. 'The Round Tower on College Green', Oct 29th 2015. https://comeheretome.com/2015/10/29/the-round-tower-on-college-green/

Ferriter, Diarmaid. 'Pope and ceremony: how the 1932 congress melded church and State.' Irish Times, Saturday, June 2nd 2012.

Fitzpatrick Dean, Joan. *'All Dressed Up: Modern Irish Historical Pageantry'*. Syracuse, NY: Syracuse University Press, 2014.

Gowen, Margaret. 'Golden Lane, Dublin 8 (04E1030)', Dublin City Archaeological Archive, Reference Code DCAA.01.26 2004-2008.

Holm, Poul. 'The Slave Trade of Dublin, Ninth to Twelfth Centuries), in Peritia 5, pp 317-345, January 1986.

Holmes, David G. 'The Eucharistic Congress of 1932 and Irish Identity', *New Hibernia Review / Iris Éireannach Nua,* Vol. 4, No. 1 (Spring, 2000), pp. 55-78.

Joyce, James. 'Ulysses'. Shakespeare and Company, Paris, 1922.

Kerr, Thomas; Harney, Lorcan; Kinsella, Jonathan; O'Sullivan, Aidan, and McCormick, Finbar, 'Early Medieval Archaeology Project (EMAP) Report 3.2 Early Medieval Dwellings and Settlements in Ireland', AD400-1100 Vol. 2: Gazetteer of Site Descriptions Version 1, Dublin, December 2009.

Little, George A. 'The Provenance of the Church of St. Michael de la Pole', Dublin Historical Record, Vol. 12, No. 1 (Feb., 1951).

Lucas, A.T. 'The Plundering and Burning of Churches in Ireland, 7th to 16th Century', in E. Rynne (ed.), North Munster Studies: Essays in commemoration of Monsignor Michael Moloney (Cork 1967).

Manning, Conleth 'Burials', in Séan Duffy (ed.), Medieval Ireland: an encyclopedia (New York, 2005).

McDonnell, E.J. Letter, Irish Independent, July 5th 1932.

Ní Mhaonaigh, Máire. 'Friend and foe: Vikings in ninth- and tenth-century Irish literature' in Howard B Clarke, Máire Ní Mhaonaigh and Raghnall Ó Floinn (eds.), Ireland and Scandinavia in the early Viking Age (Dublin, 1998), pp 381-402.

Ó Corráin, Donnchadh. 'Viking Ireland – Afterthoughts' in H.B. Clarke, M. Ní Mhaonaigh and R. Ó Floinn (eds.), *Ireland and Scandinavia in the Early Viking Age* (Dublin, 1998).

Ó Cróinín, Dáibhí. 'Early medieval Ireland: 400-1200', Essex, 1995.

O'Donovan, Edmond. 'The Irish, the Vikings and the English: new archaeological evidence from excavations at Golden Lane, Dublin' in Seán Duffy (ed.) Medieval Dublin VIII (Dublin, 2008).

O'Donovan, Edmond. 'Golden Lane, Dublin', site report. License number: 04E1030, retrieved 27/10/2018 from https://excavations.ie/report/2004/Dublin/0011672/

O'Dwyer, Rory. 'On show to the world: the Eucharistic Congress, 1932', in History Ireland, Issue 6, 2007, Vol 15.

Ó Floinn, Raghnall. 'The archaeology of the Early Viking Age in Ireland' in Howard B Clarke, Máire Ní Mhaonaigh and Raghnall Ó Floinn (eds.), Ireland and Scandinavia in the early Viking Age, Dublin, 1998.

Ó hÉailidhe, Pádraig. 'The Rathdown Slabs', *Journal of the Royal Society of Antiquaries of Ireland,* Vol. 87, No. 1 (1957), pp. 75-88.

O'Sullivan A., McCormick F., Kerr T., & Harney L. 'Early Medieval Ireland: Archaeological Excavations 1930-2004', Early Medieval Archaeological Project (EMAP), Report 2.1., UCD, December 2008.

Our History, Powers Whiskey: http://powerswhiskey.ie/our-history

Price, Neil. 'Belief and ritual' in *Vikings: Life and Legend,* London, 2014.

Robertson, John, 'Sketches of Irish History: Antiquities, Religion, Customs, and Manners', R. Groombridge, London 1844.

Strickland, Walter G. 'A Dictionary of Irish Artists', Maunsel & company, Dublin, 1913

'The Church and Round Tower of St. Michael's le Pole, Dublin', The Irish Builder, Nov 15th 1871.

Todd, J. H. (Ed) 1867. *Cogadh Gaedhel re Gallaibh: the war of the Gaedhil with the Gaill*. London.

Turner, M.K. 'Rathmichael. A Parish in the Pale', *Dublin Historical Record* Vol. 32, No. 3 (Jun., 1979).

Walsh, C. 'An early medieval roadway at Chancery Lane: from Duibhlinn to Átha Cliath?', in Sean Duffy (ed.) *Medieval Dublin IX*, Four Courts Press, Dublin, 2009.

Wyatt, David R. 'Slaves and Warriors in Medieval Britain and Ireland: 800 - 1200', Brill, 2009.

ILLUSTRATIONS

THE ENDURING MYSTERY

Round Tower at Glendalough. Image by Desi Maxwell from Pixabay. https://pixabay.com/photos/ireland-ancient-architecture-2180136/

Celtic Hand Bell (Menzies Celtic Bell of Struan) from the 'Red and White Book of Menzies', by David Prentice Menzies, Plean, Stirlingshire: Menzies, 1851.

Bell tower of the Cathedral of Ravenna by Controllore Fiscale – Public Domain. https://commons.wikimedia.org/w/index.php?curid=4740068.

SOPHIA EVANS AND THE WIDOW'S TOWER

All photos of George Evans Memorial Tower © Gerard Ronan

'Physionotrace portrait of Lady Mount Cashell' by Carl H. Pforzheimer. Collection of Shelley and His Circle, New York Public Library Digital Collections. 1801. http://digitalcollections.nypl.org/items/7581b872-4f4e-6993-e040-e00a180628a2

William Parnell by John Comerford, courtesy of National Gallery of Ireland.

Portrane Demesne by Edward Radclyffe (engraver), courtesy of the National Library of Ireland

Elizabeth Patterson Bonaparte via Wikimedia Commons https://commons.wikimedia.org/wiki/File:Elizabeth-Patterson-Bonaparte_Gilbert-Stuart_1804.jpg#file

Sydney Owenson (Lady Morgan) - from vol. 3 of *The Cabinet of Irish Literature...' Vol. 1-3.] With biographical sketches and literary notices by C. A. Read.*, by READ, Charles Anderton, (Vol. 4. by T. P. O'Connor.). Original held and digitised by the British Library. Copied from Flickr.

Bust of George Evans, © John Evans-Pritchard.

Frances Power Cobbe – image copied from 'Life of Frances Power Cobbe by Herself', Bentley, London, 1894

Saint Catherine's Church © Gerard Ronan

Evans Family Grave, Portrane © Gerard Ronan.

A SCANDAL AT LUSK

Lusk Chapel & Round Tower © Gerard Ronan

Lusk Round Tower & Church in 1791 by Grose, Captain Francis [Public domain], via Wikimedia Commons

Lusk Round Tower today © Gerard Ronan

The Famine – from 'Ridpath's history of the world: being an account of the principal events in the career of the human race from the beginnings of civilization to the present time, comprising the development of social institutions and the story of all nations' by John Clark Ridpath, 1907. Public Domain, sourced from - https://www.flickr.com/photos/internetarchivebookimages/ 14749361956/

THE HUGUENOT'S CROSS

St. Bartholomew's Day Massacre, Francois Dubois. Public Domain. https://upload.wikimedia.org/wikipedia/commons/5/52/Fr ancois_Dubois_001.jpg

Photographs of the Round Tower at Swords © Gerard Ronan

The Huguenot Cemetery on Merrion Row © Gerard Ronan

Swords Round Tower and Church by Francis Grose (1731–1791). The original uploader was Suckindiesel at English Wikipedia. (12 December 2007 (original upload date)) [Public domain], via Wikimedia Commons.

Meinhardt Schomberg – Public Domain – https://picryl.com/media/schomberg-duke-of-leinster-3rd-duke-of-schomberg-meinhard-count-of-02cbb4

Title Page of Poyntz's Prospectus from 'The present prospect of the famous and fertile island of Tobago : to the southward of Barbadoes', by Captain John Poyntz. 2nd edition, Printed by John Attwood for the author, and sold by William Staresmore, London 1695.

IRELAND'S EYE AND THE LAST ROUND TOWERS

Kilmacnessan (from a sketch by Petrie in 1828), from 'Notes on the Ecclesiastical Antiquities in the Parish of Howth, County of Dublin', by Robert Cochrane. The Journal of the Royal Society of Antiquaries of Ireland, Fifth Series, Vol. 3, No. 4 (Dec., 1893), p.399.

Garland of Howth St Mark and St Matthew, from 'Notes on the Ecclesiastical Antiquities in the Parish of Howth, County of Dublin', by Robert Cochrane. The Journal of the Royal Society of Antiquaries of Ireland, Fifth Series, Vol. 3, No. 4 (Dec., 1893).

Towers at Glendalough © Gerard Ronan

Kilmacnessan today. © Gerard Ronan

MYTH AND PROPAGANDA

Viking Monolith, by Clker-Free-Vector-Images from Pixabay. https://pixabay.com/vectors/viking-norseman-carving-monolith-30454/

Memorial plaque on Great Ship St. © Gerard Ronan

St Michael's le Pole Church, Engraving by G.A. Hanlon from a drawing by Beranger, Courtesy of National Library of Ireland.

Grave Slabs at Rathmichael © Gerard Ronan

Historical Emblems: Courtesy of Library of Congress. Reproduction Number: LC-DIG-pga-01128 (digital file from original print) LC-USZC4-1948 (color film copy transparency) http://www.loc.gov/pictures/item/92501116/

Recruiting Poster: From Library of Congress Catalog: 'The real Irish spirit' by McCaw, Stevenson & Orr, Ltd., Dublin & Belfast. Central Council for the Organization of Recruiting in Ireland, [1915]. Reproduction Number: LC-USZC4-10993 (color film copy transparency).
http://hdl.loc.gov/loc.pnp/cph.3g10993

1895 Whiskey Bottle Tower at Belfast, image Courtesy of Irish Distillers Pernod Ricard.

The Round Tower on College Green. Courtesy of Independent Newspapers/National Library of Ireland (Call No. IND H 2037).

INDEX

BY THE SAME AUTHOR...

The Irish Zorro: The Extraordinary Adventures of William Lamport

GERARD RONAN

'Ronan's book is not only an excellent history book, it is a great read. Thoroughly recommended.'
Peter Berresford Ellis. *Irish Democrat*

'Sometimes, historical biography can be a dry read. Ronan's is anything but. He provides interesting insights into the lives of large Irish enclaves in France and Spain in the first half of the 17th century along with harrowing ones of those accused of heresy and subjected to the *auto da fe* of the Inquisition. Ronan's passion and sympathy for his subject shines through so it reads like a novel. A "must-read" for the new year.'
Ann Dunne. *Irish Independent*

'The life and adventures of this pirate, heretic and spy were stranger than any fiction.'
Bookworm. *History Ireland*

ISBN-10: 086322329X
ISBN-13: 978-0863223297

William Kelly of Portrane: Forgotten Hero of the Famine and Land War

GERARD RONAN

William Kelly was a modernizing influence on Irish farming, whose tillage practices and self-invented mangelwurzel bread helped save many lives in Donabate and Portrane during the famine. A leading light in the tenants' rights leagues of the 1870s, he was a council member of the Irish Home Rule League, one of the founding fathers of the Land League and a signatory to a pivotal document of Irish history. A champion of the poor, he faded from history following his death in 1881.

ISBN-10 : 1999973828
ISBN-13 : 978-1999973827

Sophia Parnell-Evans: Feminism, Politics and Farming in 19th Century Portrane

GERARD RONAN

Sophia Parnell-Evans (1780-1853) ran a large and successful farming enterprise at a time when few women had done so. She met two Queens, the ex-wife of Napoleon and knew the radical feminist Margaret Mount Cashel. An friend of both the Darwin and Condorcet families, she was daughter and sister to three of the most prominent Irish politicians of her day, and wife to another.

A radical thinker in her own right, Sophia founded two primary schools in Donabate and had helped in no small way to mitigate the effects of the Great Famine in her locality. The memorial round tower she built in memory of her devoted husband, the MP George Evans, revived a tradition of tower building that had lain dormant for seven centuries. As the great aunt of Charles Stewart Parnell, she even made it into the pages of Joyce's "Finnegan's Wake" as the practical joker "greataunt Sophy".

ISBN-10 : 1999973879
ISBN-13 : 978-1999973872

Margaret Evans:
Poet of Portrane

GERARD RONAN

In 1798, Margaret Evans' husband, Hampden, was sentenced to hang for high treason. When his sentence was subsequently commuted to voluntary exile, she was forced to follow him to Hamburg and later to Paris, where she coped with her enforced exile and family tragedies by writing poetry for herself, her daughters and her female friends. Her writing affords us a very personal glimpse of her life as the wife of a leading United Irishman, and also the safe female space that 18th and 19th century women found in the writing and sharing of poetry. Margaret and Hampden Evans played a prominent role in the history of Portrane, and of the United Irishmen, but little was known of their story until now, or indeed of Margaret's poetry.

ISBN-10 : 1999973860
ISBN-13 : 978-1999973865